The Principles
of Aikido

Morihei Ueshiba, Founder of Aikido

The Principles of Aikido

MITSUGI SAOTOME

SHAMBHALA

Boston & Shaftesbury

1989

Photography: Glover Johns
Editor: Irene Wellington
Translators: William Gleason and Paul Kang

Shambhala Publications, Inc.
Horticultural Hall
300 Massachusetts Avenue
Boston, Massachusetts 02115

Shambhala Publications, Inc.
The Old School House
The Courtyard, Bell Street
Shaftesbury, Dorset SP7 8BP

9 8 7 6 5 4 3 2 1

First Edition

Printed in the United States of America

Distributed in the United States by Random
House and in Canada by Random House of
Canada Ltd.
Distributed in the United Kingdom by Element
Books, Ltd.

Library of Congress Cataloging-in-Publication Data
Saotome, Mitsugi.
The principles of Aikido.

Translations of Japanese text and oral lextures.

1. Aikido.   I. Title.
GV1114.35.S27   1989   796.8'154   88–34334
ISBN 0–87773–409–7

This book is dedicated,
in deep appreciation,
to all my teachers and to all of
those people all over the world
who practice Aikido and
share in its spirit.

Editor's Note

This book has been created in part from translations of Japanese text written by Saotome Sensei and in part by transcribing and formalizing oral lectures that he dictated to me. I hope that I have been able to do justice to both forms of the transmission of the substance of this book.

It has been an honor and a privilege to me to be able to help in the creation of this book. I hope that the reader will feel equally privileged at the opportunity to enjoy, understand, and apply Saotome Sensei's wisdom and his unique perspective on the study of Aikido.

Those readers who are new to, or unfamiliar with, Aikido, may want to read through the Glossary at the end of the book before beginning the text, in order to familiarize themselves with the terminology of Aikido. Others who are more familiar with the art may refer to the Glossary as needed.

Irene Wellington

Acknowledgment

All of us who took part in the creation of this book are happy to have had an opportunity to make our contribution in this effort to perpetuate the vision and art of Morihei Ueshiba O Sensei, the Founder of Aikido.

George Allica
Frank Bell
Gary Berg
Kevin Choate
William Gleason
Glover Johns
Paul Kang
David Massey
Don Moock

Hanora O'Sullivan
Ilona Popper
Fernando Salazar
Patricia Saotome
Peter Trimmer
Chuck Weber
Irene Wellington
Wendy Whited

Mitsugi Saotome

Contents

The Principles
of Aikido

1
Introduction

I worry about the conflicts that I see arise between different styles and schools of Aikido. People fight about which school is right, which one really represents O Sensei's teaching. Some of these schools seem to be trying to claim the name *Aikido* as if it were a brand name. This seems so unnecessary to me. No one can be an exact replica of O Sensei. Likewise, later generations of Aikido students cannot be identical copies of their teachers. If every person who aspires to be a teacher of Aikido tries to lay sole claim to its secrets based on superficial differences of style, what will we have? Thousands of warring schools each insisting that it alone possesses the real truth of Aikido? Where is the unity or harmony in that?

Aikido has but one principle—the universal reality of life. In their own nature as living human beings all possess the basic secret of Aikido. The purpose of Aikido is to better people's lives, to make their spirits blossom and become strong, and by making better people to make a better world. Aikido exists in this principle and this purpose, not in the style of movement or the technical details through which Aikido is taught. If the principle and the purpose are present, any technique can be Aikido. If they are absent, so is Aikido.

Many books have been published by many different Aikido instructors about Aikido technique. Some of them offer examples of ken (sword) or jo (five-foot wooden staff) kata; some give details of how empty hand kata should be done. Especially in the weapons kata, students may find that quite disparate sets of movements are presented under the same name in different books. These students may become confused. Which teacher is right? What is the correct way to do the kata? My feeling is that *all* the different ways are right—and yet none is *the* correct way.

I will present many specific techniques for both empty hand and weapons. But my purpose in including them is not to give definitive examples of kata; there are many legitimate ways to execute kata. I chose techniques that I felt illustrated important points about Aikido. After all, we are not studying to become experts in jo or hand-to-hand combat. We are not studying to become swordsmen. We are studying Aikido.

In my time as uchi deshi to O Sensei, I traveled with him to many seminars and lectures. On those occasions and during the time that I was his student, I took much ukemi for him. In the time that it was my privilege to observe his teaching he almost never taught concrete form. He was concerned with the study of budo and the spiritual meaning of Aikido, not the particulars of form. He made no distinction between empty hand and weapons techniques but switched back and forth freely between them. He wished to show the principles behind techniques and the essential thread that bound them all together. Form was merely a tool to elucidate the greater truths that were his real concern. I have tried to preserve this approach. The reader will note that many of the empty hand techniques are paired with weapons techniques that are comparable and that demonstrate the same principle. I do not wish to define technique. I wish to share with my readers my understanding of what Aikido is.

O Sensei had many uchi deshi who studied under him. They experienced his training at different times of O Sensei's life, at different stages of his training, at different places, and for various lengths of time. Each of O Sensei's uchi deshi brought his own personality and vision to his training; each has his own unique memories of O Sensei's teaching. As these uchi deshi themselves became teachers, they assimilated, preserved, and passed on the elements of O Sensei's teachings that had most impressed themselves on their memories. Many of O Sensei's students supplemented their training in Aikido with training in other arts and disciplines and used this additional knowledge to enrich their abilities in Aikido. Their personalities, their interpretation, their memories of O Sensei's teaching all combined to create their own individual styles of Aikido practice and their own methods of teaching.

But no style—no particular set of forms—is, in and of itself, Aikido. You might think of Aikido as a language. As such it has its grammar and its rules, but that grammar is very broad and accommodating. Like language, it has room for an infinite variety of creative uses of its elements and great elasticity of structure. O Sensei's dream in creating Aikido, as I understand it, was a dream of creating peace in the world, of training human aggression, of teaching people to be better human beings. I see nothing in this that prevents different styles of Aikido from coexisting and, indeed, enhancing one another in the realization of O Sensei's dream. I pray that this book will help people better understand O Sensei's in-tent in creating Aikido and will promote more unity, rather than more division, in the Aikido community. I would like to see all those who practice Aikido reaffirm that we all follow the same path in pursuit of a common goal.

In my heart, I feel that O Sensei has not died. Memories of him are indelibly imprinted on all my senses. His voice and the words he spoke still sound in my mind. His dream of peace and his love for all mankind have taken root in my soul. I offer this book in the spirit of that love to the worldwide family of Aikido in the hopes that O Sensei's dream of peace will live on and grow in them.

2

Practicing Basic Technique: Training Mental Attitude and Vision

Often, after I have demonstrated a technique in the course of teaching a class and am watching my students practice, I see them performing movements that are completely different from what I have shown them. They have not observed the subtle but essential difference between what they have seen before and what I have demonstrated. Learning to observe clearly and truly is not as easy as it may seem. Even on a purely physical level, a student's preconceptions can place blinders on his vision. If people can have such difficulty observing what is in front of their eyes, you may imagine how much more difficult it is to be receptive to the much more subtle and elusive motivations that inform the physical movement. The first task of the beginning Aikido student should be to learn to see—to observe with an open mind what his eyes tell him and to keep his spirit receptive to the deeper meaning behind technique.

I believe that training yourself in the art of perception precedes the ability to train in basic technique successfully. You must labor to hone not just your ability to clearly ob-

serve physical movement but your mental and spiritual acuity as well. You must be able to develop your intuitive sense of the intent and meaning behind the movements that your teacher demonstrates and to gain an insight into the mental and spiritual qualities that he or she possesses. I cannot overemphasize the importance of closely following the instructions of your teacher.

What you have observed, you must polish by repetition. Repetition is a great teacher and will show you your mistakes. For instance, if you are practicing suburi, or repeated cuts, with the sword, you do not have to swing the sword well if you only cut five times. To do a thousand cuts poorly is impossible; your body will tire long before you have completed them. But if you persist in your determination to do a thousand cuts without stopping, you will eventually learn the correct and efficient way to use the sword, for to perform the movement properly is the only way it is possible to accomplish such a large number of repetitions. Only through practice will your level of comprehension of

Above and opposite: Mitsugi Saotome teaching at World Headquarters, 1970.

techniques increase. Your teacher cannot an-swer through your intellect the questions of your body. To learn Aikido, you must per-form the movements you are shown again and again until your own body teaches you the natural wisdom of movement and allows you to absorb the knowledge that your in-structor gives you.

Gaining mere literal knowledge and tech-nical skill is not the goal of Aikido practice. You must work to improve your character and raise your consciousness to a higher level. The study of Aikido cannot be a selfish study. You must develop your sensitivity toward others and your concern for them in your daily interactions, both in practice and in your daily life. Such understanding must accom-pany your technical development. If you are ignorant of the effect that your actions are having on the mind and body of your part-ner, you will never realize the true purpose of practice, let alone effective technique. This is why it is so important that you never practice in such a way that you cause pain or injury to your partners. This is a moral responsibility.

An injury that you cause someone could im-pair his ability to earn his livelihood. Imag-ine, for example, the repercussions of break-ing a surgeon's fingers.

Being sensitive to the needs of others im-plies development of not only the five senses we are familiar with but the sixth and seventh senses as well. The sixth sense we might call intuition. It is the ability to see beyond the mask of your own face and catch the elusive signals that are beyond the range of the physi-cal senses. The sixth sense allows you to see *intent,* to see the action forming in the body before any move is made. It allows you to read the feelings of others.

The seventh sense is more difficult to de-scribe and to develop. "Divine inspiration" might be an equivalent term in English, but this term can also mislead. What I am think-ing of when I speak of the seventh sense is the ability to see how every action reflects the es-sential patterns that resonate through all na-ture. For example, expansion and contraction are natural functions that govern our breath-ing, and they are also principles that govern

the creation and the destruction of galaxies. In Aikido, contracting and expanding the body constitute a large part of the movement that creates successful technique. The seventh sense is the wisdom that allows us to maintain the awareness of the governing laws of nature in all things.

The seventh sense is the sense that enables you to erase the boundaries between yourself and your fellow human beings, to know that to harm another is to harm yourself, to feel the pain of others as your own pain—to sense the world as a whole entity rather than a collection of individual parts at war. Think of how you hear music. You do not listen to it note by note. You hear a whole piece and understand its beauty. The seventh sense is the ability to hear the whole music of the uni-

verse in which you participate, to hear how the note that is yours to sound fits into the song of which it is a part. Training in Aikido should strive to unite us, in both body and spirit, with the way of nature.

Developing the seventh sense helps to ensure that your relationship to your practice partners will be fruitful. Your practice partners come to you with a great variety of experience. They are of different ages, professions, and temperaments. No two come with the same physique, the same character, or the same way of thinking. This seems simple but is often forgotten. It is important to remain constantly aware of each of your partners' different abilities and limitations.

Our practice is not a realistic battle but a contrived situation that gives us the opportunity to polish ourselves both physically and spiritually. Our partner is not our enemy. Partners provide each other with the chance to face a hypothetical attack and resolve its problems. Uke's attack must be sincere and without malicious intent—just pure. Nage, in turn, must never inflict injury or show disrespect to uke, who has put himself in nage's power. To become angry or emotional or to attempt to injure your partner intentionally is not just a breach of etiquette. It is destructive to you as well as to your partner and very foolish. In my years as an instructor, I have witnessed many whose potential and abilities were wasted because of conceit and failure to see their fellow human beings truly. They refused to see their partners' physical limitations and ignored the vast possibilities that exist beyond those limitations. Physical development may stop as a person ages, but spiritual growth should never cease. Those who fail to understand this are the ones who lose their direction in life and lose the way of Aikido. To my sorrow I have seen many fall even at very advanced stages of training.

You must not succumb to anger, hatred, fears of your inferiority, arrogance, or other negative feelings in practice or in your life. Become a crystal mirror that reflects your life. Selfishness and conceit will cloud the surface of that mirror. You must remain humble and receptive, keeping in mind that the purpose of your practice is to improve yourself and to elevate your consciousness, not to compete or compare yourself with others. Practicing with unpleasant inner feelings and negative emotions obscures your inner vision and hinders you from seeing clearly what is happening around you. You will lose your sixth sense, that intuitive sense vital to seeing the imminent moves of your partners. You will lose the seventh sense of the link between the pattern and purpose of your practice and the patterns

of nature. All things follow the path of nature, and Aikido is no exception. If your practice of Aikido becomes separated from this path, you will not be able to sustain the creative energy that allows you to progress in your training.

Of course, it is necessary to become strong; but physical, mental, and spiritual strength must all grow together. Aikido is a way of balance. A person with a strong body and a diseased or criminal mind is a menace to society. A person with a sound mind but poor health will have difficulty coping with the demands of reality. We must strive, in the long and difficult process of training, to achieve balance between body and mind and also balance *within* our minds and bodies. Emotional stability, physical equilibrium, and spiritual equanimity—these are the goals toward which our training is aimed.

Training with this intent helps us learn to look calmly on the changes and reverses of the economic and the material world. Real happiness lies beyond the turmoil of the world. We are bound by the laws of nature and of God, but within the law of natural selection exists the principle of evolution and adaption to the influences that surround us. Man's distinguishing quality is his great ability to adapt. By fully and humbly adapting to and accepting the laws of the universe, we liberate and place ourselves above animal strife. The key that looses us from its chains lies in the principle of evolution.

Like evolution, the study of Aikido is a long, slow, gradual process. Just as the mountaineer achieves the mountain top step by step, you must also approach your practice one step at a time. You must scrupulously review each step that brings you forward. The mountaineer, having gained a foothold, checks to make sure that it is secure before depending it to lift him to the next. Do not let temporary setbacks or failures discourage you. Aikido is progress, growth, and change, and some errors are inevitable. You will never reach a stage where you can say that you have finished your study, that you have "learned" Aikido. Just as life's lessons continue until your death, so should your training continue to develop as long as you practice. Patience, as well as hard work, is necessary to your training.

I would like, finally, to present for your contemplation the following excerpt from Morihei Ueshiba O Sensei's book, *Budo,* written in 1938. These are rules written especially for those entering the dojo for the first time.

PRECEPTS FOR PRACTICE TO BE UNDERSTOOD AND DEEPLY CONSIDERED

1. The original purpose of budo was to send a man to death with a single blow. For this reason you must obey your teacher implicitly in practice and never engage in competition.
2. The original budo is a study by which the individual connects to the whole. Therefore, you must practice with complete awareness of all that surrounds you. You should maintain this awareness along with a healthy degree of tension at all times.
3. You should always practice in the spirit of joy.
4. Your teacher can only give you an outline, a hint here and there to guide you. Only through constant practice will you master the practical use of this mystery. Learn to understand with your body. Do not engage in a futile effort to learn a great number of techniques but rather study the techniques one by one and make each one your own.
5. One should begin daily practice with proper warm-up exercises. This will strengthen the body and prevent undue stress on it. The first ten minutes of practice should be less rigorous than the practice that follows. There is no reason for injury, even to older people. Remember that your practice should be joyful.

You must gain an understanding of the real purpose of your training.
6. The original budo is training in the spirit of harmony. Its purpose is to produce real human beings who will improve the world. The techniques are secret teachings and show the secret principle of budo. They should not be disclosed to the public indiscriminately, especially not to those who might misuse this understanding.

Keep these rules in mind as you read the rest of this book. The meaning of some of them may not be clear to you now, but as you continue your reading and your practice, their meaning and their importance will become apparent. They form a context within which the principles of Aikido must be considered.

Koki: Self-challenge

Application of Irimi-Tenkan

3

Musubi

Aikido is the study of wisdom. If you cannot control and trust yourself—if you cannot see yourself clearly—you will never have any knowledge or trust of others and you certainly will not be able to control them. The purpose of Aikido training is not to create aggressive fighters but to refine wisdom and self-control. As a student of Aikido, you must study to improve and polish yourself, not to compete with others.

The key to this process—and the heart of Aikido—is musubi. This word translates loosely into English as "unity," or "harmonious interaction." In practice, musubi means the ability to blend, both physically and mentally, with the movement and energy of your partner. Musubi is the study of good communication. In any interaction between people, communication exists, whether acknowledged or not. It is up to the participants in the interaction to determine whether the communication will be productive or useless, friendly or hostile, true or inaccurate. Musubi, as it is refined, can mean the ability to control and alter interaction, changing a hostile approach to a healthy encounter or an attack into a handshake.

Musubi is both a method of learning and the goal of study. Musubi, in its ultimate refinement, relates to the achievement of a sense of universal harmony and, in technique, the ability to control encounters for the good. But can such ability be achieved by forcing, coercing, or frightening a person into learning it? No. Musubi must be taught and studied according to the principles it exemplifies

so that the Aikido student's consciousness may be refined along with his physical movement. Musubi must be taught through good interaction and firm but kindly guidance.

Learning to respond to attacks with musubi is a long and difficult process. One cannot strike at a beginner and tell him, "Don't fight! Blend, blend!" The beginner will not blend but will react with fear and aggression, the instinctive reactions to threat. The begin-

Musubi: Harmony

ner will attempt to defend him- or herself by struggling or by hurting the attacker.

In Aikido the goal is to tame and control these animal instincts, not stimulate them. This is why, especially for beginners, we often use various kinds of grabs as attacks. The beginning student is not equipped to deal with real attacks—like strikes or kicks—with either mental calm or proper physical movement. Grabs allow the beginner to study techniques without fear for physical safety's interfering with learning the correct responses. Instead of engaging in struggle and competition, the student polishes both movement and mind. The student studies control—of him- or herself, of the partner, and of the relationship between them. Grabs have the advantage of providing a physical contact between practice partners so that both may be able to feel what makes a movement work. If there is no physical contact, beginning students will find it hard to explore the mechanics of technique.

Practice for beginners may often start with static grabs. These allow the study of correct posture, footwork, and body position. Students may then progress to moving grabs, which allow the development of a sense of timing and distance and the exploration of the spatial relationships between them and their partners. Students can begin learning to adjust to various degrees and kinds of force, speed, and direction. They can start to build confidence in their ability to communicate with their partners, to build up their intuitive senses of their partners' movements and intents.

Cooperation is very important in Aikido training. Almost all practice is done with a partner, and the relationship between partners must be a manifestation of musubi. Both nage and uke bear this responsibility. While nage must train to blend with, rather than

struggle against, attacks, uke must learn to attack in a way that is appropriate to the technique being studied and to provide the proper conditions for learning. In a simple example, if the teacher has demonstrated a technique involving a forward throw, it is appropriate for uke to push forward. If instead uke pulls backward, attempting to thwart nage's technique, this will only reduce practice to a struggle and neither student will learn how the technique works. Advanced students can benefit from unexpected attacks, free practice, and attempts at reversals, but this is after years of studying basic techniques and learning what conditions require what actions.

The study of Aikido is the study of wisdom, and wisdom, in large part, is the possession of common sense. Common sense, unfortunately, is much rarer than its name would imply. In this world it is lost or never learned. Training in musubi and the basic principles of Aikido involves relearning common sense. We find evidence of this in the basic defensive movements if irimi and tenkan. These two movements can also be spoken of as one movement irimi-tenkan, as yin and yang are parts of a whole.

Both irimi and tenkan are movements that people use in everyday life without thinking. Imagine that you are walking down a crowded city street with the general flow of pedestrian traffic, and you see someone coming directly toward you, walking in the opposite direction. Would you rapidly back into the people walking behind you to get out of the way? No, you would continue to walk toward him and perhaps turn sideways as he reached you to let him pass by. This is an example of irimi. Now imagine that the same person pushes into you while passing by. Would you grab him and cling to keep your balance? No, you might spin around to keep your balance and keep walking. This is tenkan. Both movements are simple, natural examples of common sense. Anybody can do them, and their very simplicity and universality confirms their truth.

But the person untrained in Aikido who sees someone coming toward him or her with an attack automatically does what the same person knows to be foolish on the crowded street—tries to walk backward. When a push is a hostile gesture, the person either freezes or grabs onto the assailant for balance. The person loses common sense and ability to perceive the natural reaction. On the crowded street a person shows an understanding of musubi; faced with threat, the mind regresses toward fear and aggression, and the body loses its ability to react with agility and efficiency.

Aikido training, through its gradual and cooperative process, teaches how to apply the principles of musubi to increasingly difficult situations. It trains your mind to retain its calm and your vision to retain its clarity so that fear, anger, or lack of confidence do not distort your body movement. It trains your body so that it is supple and responsive; constant practice supplies the body with the wisdom of experience. In this way, the body becomes the reflection and the physical manifestation of your mind. Body and mind working together—again in the relationship of musubi—allows you to react simply and efficiently and sensibly under pressure, rather than letting yourself be dominated and controlled by circumstances.

One sees advanced students in Aikido striking at and throwing each other very hard, but they have been brought to this point in their training by careful stages that educate the mind along with the body. Thus the hard attacks become a challenge rather than an assault. The purpose of striking and kicking in practice becomes not an attempt to destroy an enemy but a means of discovering your own and your partner's strength, balance, intuition, and mental stability. Instead of facing each other with distrust, fear, and competitiveness, you meet your practice partners with concentration, sincerity, and a sense of enjoyment.

Please recall the examples that I gave of how irimi and tenkan operate automatically as part of your reactions to situations in your everyday life. Another important feature of musubi is operating in your encounter on that crowded street. As you meet the pedestrian who is walking toward you, your reactions reflect and respond to the other person's, rather than conflicting with them. The conjunction of you and the other pedestrian represents a continuous and smooth flow of energy, a give and take of force and direction. This is another—and perhaps the most important—element of musubi, namely, learning to feel and use the unity of energy.

This is why kokyu tanden ho, as O Sensei said, is the most fundamental training in musubi. Kokyu tanden ho is not a fighting technique at all but a study in physical relationship and movement. In this exercise, two partners sit opposite each other in seiza, with uke grabbing nage. Nage, using the whole body as a coordinated unit, attempts to unbalance uke. The purpose of kokyu tanden ho is to discover the principle of circular energy. As uke firmly grasps nage's wrists and provides resistance, nage receives the energy that uke gives him and returns it through uke's center of balance. All parts of nage must act in unity. Nage must meet uke's grab extended, with his arms acting like a spring, so that he can recoil and again extend. He must breathe in as uke grabs and breathe out as he returns uke's force. His mind must remain flexible and receptive.

Kokyu tanden ho is a noncompetitive exercise, not a contest of strength. Uke provides enough resistance to challenge nage but not so much as to make execution of the technique impossible. Nage does not struggle to throw uke but uses this training to study balance, breathing, and unity of physical and mental energy. However, as your training advances, you will find that your partner's physical strength can work to your advantage. Because kokyu tanden ho works on the principle of musubi, on absorbing and returning energy, the effect is that uke and nage *combine* energies. Nage has the use of both his own and uke's strength. The more uke resists and uses his strength, the greater the tool that nage has at his disposal. This circularity of energy is the essence of musubi.

You should apply the principles of musubi that you learn through practicing kokyu tanden ho to all your Aikido techniques. It is musubi that will allow you to reach the point where physical size and strength make no difference in your ability to execute technique. If you fail to grasp the principles of musubi and to put them into practice, you will always be at the mercy of the strength of others and will always be in danger of reverting to competitive struggle.

O Sensei said again and again to his students that the same principles that govern nature govern Aikido. A small bird may fly in a gale, but not by struggling against the wind. It must use the force of the wind to aid it. You may successfully pilot a small boat in rough seas, but only if you know how to ride the waves. So too in Aikido, the student seeks to learn to receive force and transform it into his ally rather than to fight it. This is wisdom,

and this is the reality of musubi.

As you continue to train, your ability to use the principles of musubi should expand. The beginner needs physical contact to be able to feel the connection between himself and his partner. The advanced student learns to maintain that connection with less and less physical contact. Some techniques may eventually be executed with no physical contact at all. Daily training increases your ability to relate not only to the people with whom you practice, but to all others as well, because it expands your vision, your intuition, and your sensitivity. In your life outside of practice there may be less opportunity for physical contact with others, but the lessons of your training can and should be applied to the benefit of your relations with others and to mankind as a whole. The process of removing your blinders and allowing your consciousness to grow and become ever more inclusive should never cease.

Finally, remember that to achieve musubi in your practice you must establish relationships of trust with your practice partners. Without trust, you cannot train in Aikido. Old-style bujutsu developed very capable fighters but did not necessarily promote enlightened minds. More often, since the students of bujutsu were essentially punished into proficiency, it developed in them a distrustful and paranoid consciousness, a street fighter's mentality. The purpose of Aikido, on the contrary, is to raise the spirit and refine it—to gain strength through wisdom, not brutality. This is why the *process* of Aikido training is so important. Through gradually educating the Aikido student and refining his ability to meet the demands of severe training, the meaning of that training is changed. Hard strikes and hard falls are no longer instruments of threat but tools that improve the Aikido student's abilities. The difference between old-style bujutsu and Aikido in the effect of the severity of training is like the difference between a fire that rages out of control and the fire of a forge. One destroys, distorts, and kills; the other, while equal in heat and in intensity, improves raw metal, shapes it, and turns it into a thing of beauty. Aikido students must always remember that the purpose of their training is to challenge and improve themselves rather than to intimidate their partners or to indulge their own egos at their partner's expense.

It is these qualities of trust, cooperation, open-mindedness, and generosity in the practice of Aikido that allow its students to relinquish the fears that limit them and inhibit their ability to interact with others and to gain the confidence and trust in themselves that will enable them to gain the harmonious connection with others that is musubi. Without musubi, Aikido is not Aikido but just another way of fighting.

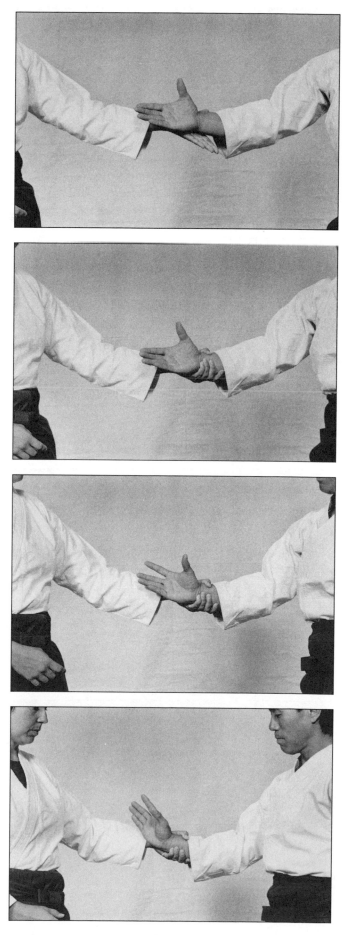

Musubi (detail). This close-up allows you to examine the subtlety of movement that allows musubi to succeed. As uke grabs nage, nage absorbs the power of her attack, but observe how small the retraction of his arm and body are before he begins to return the force of her attack to her. Nage retracts just enough to prompt uke into continuing her pressure but not enough to allow her to push him back. Hand, shoulder, and hip rotate together. Nage begins this movement with his hand upward, palm open, in order to receive uke's energy. As uke presses in, he rotates his hand in concert with his body so that his palm turns toward uke and presses toward her center. The human body functions on stimulus and response. As uke feels that nage is yielding in response to her pressure, she will continue that pressure and continue to feed him the energy required to execute this movement. If nage attempts to stop her movement, she will also stop her attack or retract it. The exercise depicted here is a study in how nage's response to uke's attack can in turn direct uke's response to nage. (Uke: Wendy Whited)

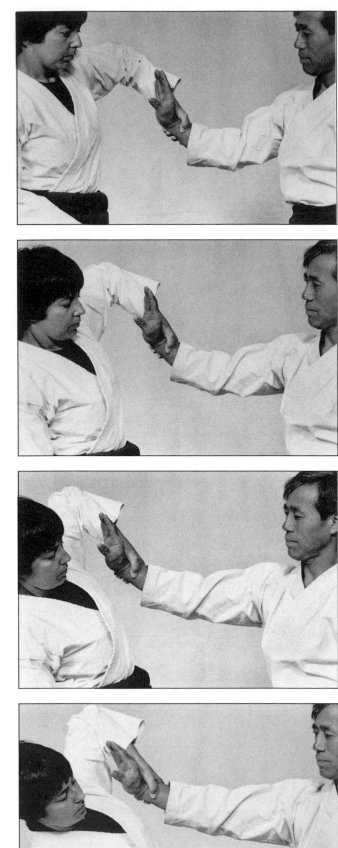

Musubi. In order to execute this movement successfully not only your body but your mind must be properly attuned to uke. The mental state of nage is hard to depict in photographs, but it is worthwhile to observe the calm on nage's face. He does not exhibit aggression or greed for success but receives the input from his uke impartially. In order to train properly in musubi, you must be completely receptive to your uke's movement. The mechanics of this technique are simple, but the required harmonizing of all physical and mental systems requires long training and the development of acute sensitivity to achieve. One of the most important benefits of this exercise is that acquiring a physical understanding of it will change your mental vision. Conversely, as your mental vision begins to change and improve, your physical perception and performance will alter to suit your mind. This interchange should be an integral feature of your study of Aikido. Training in musubi, in irimi-tenkan principle, and in kokyu tanden ho should be lifelong studies, as important to advanced students as they are to the beginner. They are the keys to developing a peaceful and receptive mind, which in turn will promote good understanding of the art of Aikido. (Uke: Wendy Whited)

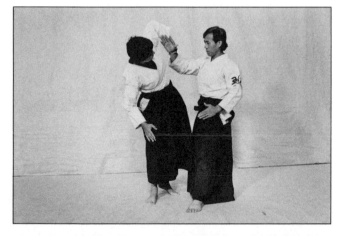

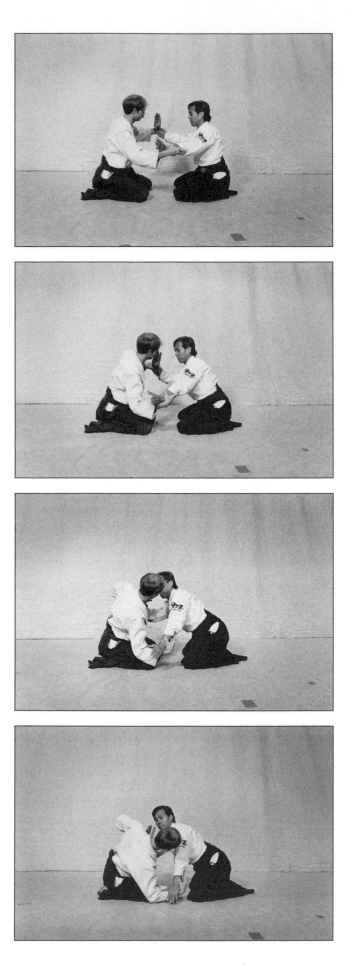

Kokyu tanden ho. This exercise provides important training in musubi, or harmonious communication, which is essential to good Aikido. Nage does not passively wait for uke to grab but offers his hands extended. As uke grabs, nage absorbs uke's pressure with both of his hands and his body. You will note that the change in nage's body position in the second picture of this series is very slight; he does not distort or disturb his center of balance. After absorbing uke's pressure, nage returns it to him, distributing it outwards and away from uke's center. Observe how nage's hands and body move in concert throughout the entire movement and how nage follows uke as uke goes down. At no time during this movement is nage overextended and pushing solely with his arms. There is a circular movement of nage's arms as he draws uke's energy and returns it. (Uke: Chuck Weber)

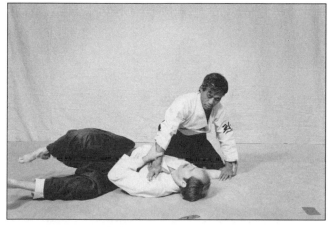

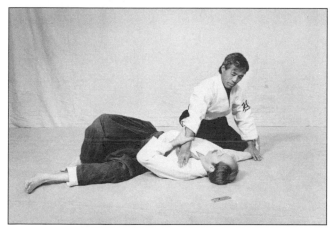

Kokyu tanden ho. Here uke grabs nage's wrists from below. In order to establish the connection with his partner that will allow him to execute this exercise, nage first opens his hands outward. If he tried to push straight in, uke would be able to force nage's arms upward. By opening his arms outward, nage splits uke's strength and concentration. Nage empties uke's center, which gives him the space for entry. (Uke: Chuck Weber)

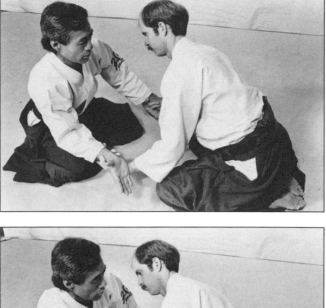

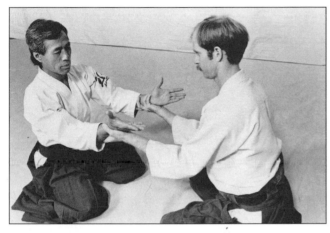

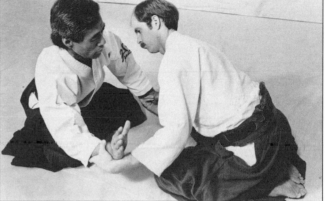

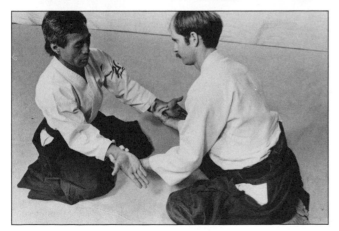

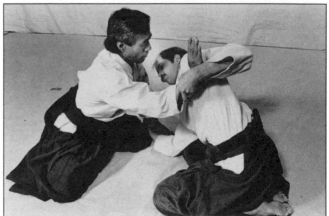

Kokyu tanden ho. Both relaxation and stability are essential to the successful execution of kokyu tanden ho. Nage must be firm and centered but not stiff. Breathing must be relaxed and coordinated with body movements. Kokyu tanden ho also provides a good opportunity for uke to learn the feeling of falling and rolling in a non-anxiety-provoking situation. Uke can also learn how it feels to follow nage's movement correctly. (Uke: Chuck Weber)

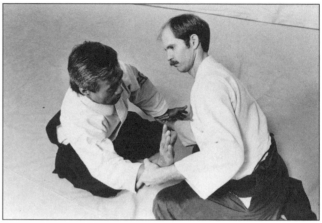

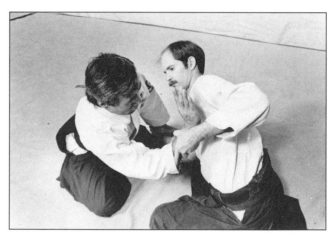

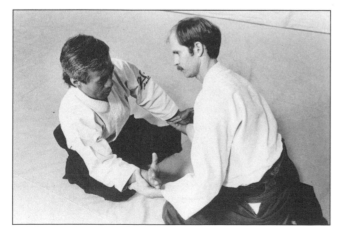

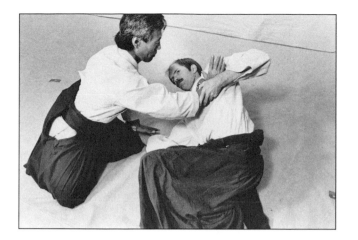

Shomenuchi iriminage. This version of shomenuchi irimi-nage provides an illustration of the principles of musubi and of kokyu tanden ho at a more advanced level. Uke's attack is a strike, not a grab, and nage never grabs uke. The contact between nage and uke is less physical here and more dependent upon timing, distance, and mental connection. In this technique the ukemi reflects nage's movement, and the throw reflects uke's movement. Nage tries to compress uke. Uke resists the compression and tries to regain his posture and stability. As uke rises, so does nage, who continues the rising motion in a sweeping upward spiral that takes nage's feet out from under him. Note the similarity of nage's hand movements to those used in kokyu tanden ho. (Uke: Don Moock)

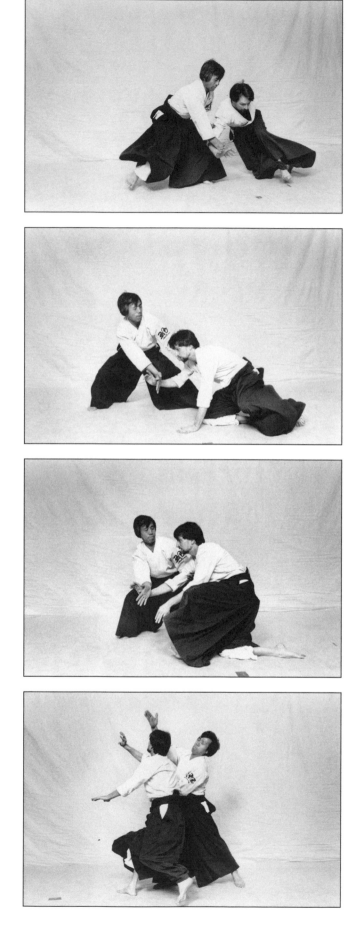

4
Ukemi

The practice of Aikido requires the presence of a partner. A few exercises may be done in isolation to hone your strength or technical skills, but the key to good training lies in the interaction between uke and nage. Some people incorrectly simplify the definitions of *uke* and *nage* to "attacker" and "defender." Such simplification is misleading as to the true nature and importance of the roles of nage and uke. More correctly, nage means "the one who throws" and uke means "the one who receives the force." If you think in terms of attacker and defender, it is likely that you will regard the role of nage, the one who is attacked and who executes the technique, as the important role, and the role of uke as merely giving the nage a body on which to practice his technique. Nothing could be further from the truth.

Ukemi is the art of being uke, and the quality of nage's practice depends on how well uke has learned this art. Ukemi involves creating the conditions that make a given technique appropriate, responding correctly to nage's movements, and taking whatever fall concludes the technique. In short, uke is responsible for creating the conditions that allow nage to learn. If uke has no sense of the effects of a technique, no resilience, or no responsiveness to nage's movements or if he is fearful or awkward at falling, nage will not be able to study the technique effectively.

In practicing any technique, partners will alternate taking the roles of nage and uke. You must not regard the time that you spend in the role of uke as merely marking time between your turns at being nage but as a learning opportunity of importance equal to or greater than the time you spend in the role of nage. In fact, those who excel at taking ukemi will most likely excel in technique also, for they will be able to absorb knowledge through their bodies of how a properly executed technique feels, as well as absorbing knowledge through their minds. Developing good ukemi is the shortest path to acquiring skill in Aikido.

Many elements make up good ukemi. The first is musubi. You must have good communication with your nage, both physical and intuitive. If you are insensitive to the movements or intentions of your partner, you will hamper your partner's practice and risk injuring yourself. A good uke does not anticipate the partner's moves but hones his perception to the point where reactions are instinctive and intuitive, rather than solely dependent upon physical manipulation.

Learning ukemi is learning to protect your body from injury; you must be constantly flexible and alert. You should be able to take a fall from any angle at any unexpected moment. Such skill leads to the mastery of advanced techniques. You should also learn to take ukemi when holding bokken and jo. The weapons training in Aikido includes some techniques in which one partner disarms the other. Many of these include throws and the uke should be prepared for this. Learning to protect yourself through ukemi is also your responsibility to your fellow students. While nage should be aware of uke's limitations and refrain from unnecessary roughness, your partners have a right to expect a degree of proficiency in your ukemi commensurate with your level of advancement. If your ukemi ability falls behind your ability in techniques as you advance, you will hinder your partners' practice. You may also be placing too much of the burden of your own safety on your partners, especially as you begin to practice the more demanding techniques. Your own training, too, will suffer, for you will never be able to practice the more difficult techniques with full intensity.

Taking ukemi does not mean that you are playing the role of the loser. It is a study in communication and perception and in self-protection. Further still, it is a means of retaining control over yourself and over your circumstances. This aspect of ukemi becomes apparent in advanced training, when practice goes beyond techniques involving a single attack followed by a throw to those involving multiple attacks and reversals. (See the three kaeshiwaza photograph series in chapter 13.) The sensitivity and awareness to nage that allow you to be a good uke also give you the ability to see the weakness in nage's technique and to recognize the points where nage is open. If you are a good uke, you can take advantage of these and make a good recovery or a reversal. If you have not learned good ukemi, you will not be able to retain enough balance or control to do either.

Learning good ukemi, of course, takes time and a lot of practice. As a beginner, you will be introduced to the concept of ukemi slowly. After you have been introduced to irimi and tenkan movement, you will start to practice rolling and falling. This should happen before you begin practicing basic technique. When you begin to practice basic technique, your study will be based on kata. The kata give students a framework in which to study and explore the workings of different move-

ments and perfect their execution. You must master the kata before you can make more creative use of Aikido movement and become more elastic in your ukemi. Jiuwaza, in which you are expected to respond spontaneously to different attacks and throws, should be reserved for more advanced students. As your training progresses, always remember that the key to gaining the ability for spontaneous and creative technique lies in good ukemi.

During my time as an uchi deshi, I was reprimanded for taking inferior ukemi. O Sensei's comments, as I remember them, may be summarized as follows:

1. Do not try to anticipate what is to come. An overcalculating mind will obscure the body's responses and cause it to lag. This will force you to take unnatural ukemi, which in turn will be reflected in technique training, hindering your improvement.
2. Observe your partner's movement and catch his intention. This is part of ukemi training.
3. Do not forget the relevance of ukemi training to everyday life. All prominent people who achieve something of value in everyday life have absorbed the principles of ukemi. The journey through life is beset by many hardships. Success comes to those who resolve their difficulties with the flexibility and open-mindedness of ukemi. Those who force their ukemi in an unnatural manner in practice will see no positive results from their training in their life.
4. It is simple wisdom to avoid injury and strive for the goal of your choice, whether in the dojo or in everyday life.
5. An open and supple mind, a flexible body, modesty, and sincerity—these are the necessary elements in the art of ukemi. Without them, ukemi training fails. Without ukemi, waza training will never come to fruition.

Observe O Sensei's words regarding the relevance of ukemi to everyday life. Ukemi nurtures your ability to sense what is coming, to analyze a circumstance and to respond quickly. Just as those who anticipate too much in their ukemi in practice often fail to see the direction of a technique, those who are too calculating in life often fail to observe what is happening around them. They have no flexibility in responding to difficulties in life because they cannot see them until they are within their grip. Good ukemi training will allow you to see the future truly because your vision will be based on observation and intuition, rather than an arbitrary decision made in advance of the evidence. Good ukemi represents the same wisdom as that of the fisherman who through long experience can sense what the coming weather will be.

Ukemi training has great physical merit; it strengthens the body and increases its flexibility. Also, the more comfortable you become with your ukemi, the more fun your practice becomes. I remember O Sensei's joy in practice, his warmth and his humor. To have pleasure in your practice need not spoil your concentration; you can relax and yet be serious. One can hardly overstate the importance of ukemi training and of its contribution to your practice and your life.

Mitsugi Saotome taking ukemi for O Sensei

5

The Sword and the Spirit of Ikkyo

The Life of Blood and the Blood of Life

The history of the sword and swordsmanship in Japan is a model for the dilemma of budo that Aikido addresses: How can a martial art become a tool for peace? On the one hand, the story of the samurai in Japan is a story of blood, death, and cruelty. On the other hand, out of the bloody turmoil came some of the most peaceful and enlightened men in the history of Japan. Destruction and chaos gave birth to a philosophy of communion with the divine principles of the universe and of love for fellow men.

This is not so great a contradiction as it sounds. What man is more likely to know the true value of life than one who knows the reality of death? Who is more likely to realize the moral destitution of conflict, bloodshed, the vicious cycles of revenge and retaliation, and the power struggles they engender than a man who was immersed in those things? Certainly, there are many who have philosophized about the evils of war and recognized its futility from a distance, but often their ideas have not been informed by a true knowledge of those evils. They did not know their enemy; therefore, when their theories were put to the test, their enemy proved stronger.

Amid the spiritual poverty of war, then, we find some of the richest understandings of the way to peace. This spiritual awareness was bought at the cost of a great deal of suffering and a great many lives. Most of those who followed the way of the sword remained embroiled in conflict and deadly combats. They were unable to free themselves from the fear of death and of the repercussions that their own violent actions might bring upon them. Inherent in the training to become a great swordsman and warrior, however, were concepts that contained the keys to escape from their entanglement in conflict and bloodshed.

To understand how this could come about, we must bear in mind the concept of yin and yang: each idea or action implies its opposite, and the union of these opposites creates the true whole. The most basic illustration of this is life and death. Life and death appear to be opposites, yet neither is complete without the other. All things that live must eventually die; death is a part of life. A world where there is no death is a world where there is no life; only things that do not live do not die.

The swordsman who was trained in dealing out death did not kill purely for the sake of killing. He killed to protect something he valued—his own life, his honor, his lord, his people, or all of these things. The art of the swordsman was thus dedicated to the accomplishment of two opposing ideas—the preservation and the destruction of life.

In order to achieve success at his dual goal,

Ikkyo omote in the Sarasota dojo (Uke: Shigeru Suzuki; photograph by P. Saotome)

Mitsugi Saotome taking ukemi for O Sensei (Photograph by Doshu Kisshomaru Ueshiba)

the swordsman had to develop a consciousness that supported yet another contradiction. He had to have a commitment to his purpose that was so great that his own life was of no value in comparison. He would willingly sacrifice his own life to achieve his enemy's death. This is the principle of ai uchi, or "mutual destruction." However, if a man truly achieved this state of mind, this great degree of determination and resolve where his own death was a matter of indifference to him, he paradoxically gained a greater chance at life. The consciousness of ai uchi put a confrontation on a level where strength and weakness have no meaning. Each person's life and death are equal, and life and death are the

only questions at stake. Also, if a swordsman willingly accepts the inevitability of his own death, he is relieved of the fear of death. He can proceed free of all doubt and full of determination.

The consciousness of ai uchi cannot be achieved through a disregard for the value of life. It can only be achieved by becoming aware of the true value of life. A person cannot truly give up his life without knowing its worth; if he courts death without appreciating his life, unacknowledged regrets and longings may assail him and cause him to panic. Nor can a person truly desire an opponent's death without knowing the value of what it is that he desires. The swordsman's willingness to die can only come about by his rising above the attachment to life, not by ignoring its precious gift.

Thus the swordsman, in his pursuit of death, is forced to come to terms with life. In his attempts to preserve life, he is forced to achieve a calm acceptance of death. In his acceptance of death, he achieves an inner serenity and determination that help him to retain life, and in his lack of attachment to life he gains a greater understanding of its meaning. Such was the concept of ai uchi.

Ai uchi, however, is still a philosophy geared toward destruction and death. Some swordsmen were able to transcend the limitations of ai uchi and achieve an even greater wisdom and internal serenity. One such man was Harigaya Sekiun, a great swordsman who lived in the seventeenth century. He realized that strength and skill, no matter how great, did not guarantee mental peace or physical safety. He wrote:

> Those who are less than I, I will defeat. Those whose ability is greater than mine will defeat me. If my opponent and I are of a similar ability, *ai uchi* will occur. This is the height of ignorance and foolishness. It employs the same tactics and mentality as that of beasts, that of tigers, wolves, and other wild things fighting for survival. I completely renounce this way. This is not the way of the sword, nor should it be the behavior of human beings.

While many others regarded ai uchi as an attitude of enlightenment, Harigaya Sekiun obviously did not. He felt that no man would willingly give up his valuable life, the instinct to survive was too deeply a part of his nature. Sekiun pointed to the history of human civilization as evidence. Faced with a life-and-

Satsu jin ken: The killing of one's enemy

death situation, a man would always wish to be the victor.

Sekiun introduced the concept of ai nuke or mutual preservation of life. To achieve ai nuke, he said, a person must enter into the realm of mu, the eternal void. He must gain an understanding of the universal principle behind all life, and strive toward a love that embraced all life. The lust for one's own life and the attachment to victory he saw as a narrow understanding of the value of life. To use Sekiun's own words:

> The way of the sword is rooted in the consciousness of the sage. It is contained in such a mentality. There is but one path, although it

Katsu jin ken: The saving of one's enemy

Kurai dori: To control your enemy's spirit

may take many forms. On this point, the sages of both ancient and modern times agree. Because of this concurrence of minds, the sage also has no thought as to who is greater or lesser. If two sages meet in a situation of confrontation, the result will inevitably be *ai nuke*.

Kazumi Ise no Kami Nobutsena, the founder of the Shin Kage Ryu sword school, voiced a similar view:

To defeat evil or protect oneself from harm is merely a corollary to the goal of martial arts. Absolute freedom from attachment and desire is the state of mind for which one should aim. To approach even a step toward such a goal,

one must attempt to learn the divine purpose of life. One must possess the sword of wisdom and learn to be at one with the universe. In doing this, one may come to find the true meaning of bu in the divine realm.

The swordsmen who achieved this degree of enlightenment engaged in many battles and endured much hardship before they reached this consciousness. Sekiun fought over fifty battles with the sword and survived. The hard experiences of war taught these men the spiritual emptiness of combat. In the midst of death, they discovered the beauty of life. They learned that satsu jin ken, "the killing of the enemy," was equivalent to spiritual suicide. Katsu jin ken, "the saving of the enemy's life," was the only true victory, the only way of saving the integrity of one's own life.

This concept of budo, the possession of a love of all life so great that it allows you to love your enemy and the spiritual strength to put that love into practice, lies at the philosophical heart of Aikido. Its physical and practical manifestation is the principle of ikkyo.

Ikkyo: Weapon of the Spirit

To become a warrior who follows the path of budo is no easy thing. Ai nuke, "mutual preservation," and katsu jin ken, "the saving of your enemy's life," both imply that you have the power of choice. If you are completely at the mercy of others, you will never be able to determine the course of an encounter. You can never save your own life or the lives of those you wish to protect nor can you save your enemy from burdening his soul with your destruction. To practice *ai nuke* you must have great strength.

I am not talking of the concept of "peace through strength" with which many modern leaders justify insane nuclear proliferation. I am talking of the inner strength that allows a person to retain courage and calm in the face of danger and disorder. Perhaps you will understand what I mean if I say that a man like Mahatma Gandhi embodies the spirit of budo and is an example of a true warrior, much more so than many modern military men. He used no weapons but his serene and invincible spirit and his courage. Time and time again, he offered his life as a sacrifice to save and improve the lives of others. And over and over his enemies, faced with his courage and forced to examine their own consciences, could not allow him to die but submitted to his will. His lack of attachment

to his own life was not founded on a disregard for life, but on a deep appreciation of its preciousness. He dedicated his own life to improving the lives of others. It is not the weapon that he wields that creates the warrior, it is the spirit with which he wields it.

This is the basic principle of ikkyo, kurai dori, to take control of your enemy's spirit. Ikkyo means "first technique"; it also refers to the "first instant." The essence of ikkyo lies in the concept of taking control of an encounter from the first moment, not in the specific movements used to execute it. In the many series of photographs that portray ikkyo in this book, you will see many varieties of movement, performed both with weapons and with empty hands. All, however, have in common that the defender controls the attacker's center from the beginning of the movement.* Once you have control, you have the power of choice: to injure or protect your attacker. The choice of Aikido is to protect. A choice is also offered to the attacker. This is clearly seen in the manifestation of ikkyo known as ichi no tachi. In ichi no tachi, both partners are armed with swords. It describes a variety of techniques in which the defender achieves a position where he controls the attacker's life with one movement. In one of the versions shown, as the attacker raises his sword to strike, the defender brings his sword up to point at the attacker's throat. At this point, the attacker has two choices: to give up the conflict or to die. The defender offers the attacker life rather than imposing death. If the attacker continues to try to fight at this point, he is

---

* *Uke* and *nage* are not appropriate terms for sword techniques. In addition, when you and your partner are armed, the line between winner and loser becomes much less ambiguous. Nevertheless, the creative relationship between uke and nage described in chapter 4 still applies here.

committing suicide.

The most important element of ikkyo is the spirit. No weapon or technical expertise will make ikkyo work if your confidence and courage do not inform them. You must enter and take over your enemy's spirit with the fearlessness embodied by the principle of irimi. Yet your fearlessness must be tempered by the principle of ai nuke. You must pass beyond the desire to defeat your opponent and reach toward the goal of ending the conflict before it starts.

The most important purpose in studying ikkyo is in its application to your daily life. We are not training in Aikido to become master swordsmen or experts in hand-to-hand combat. But to develop the consciousness of a master swordsman will stand you in good stead. To learn to face each encounter in life with courage and serenity, to put your whole self into each challenge as if it might be the last one of your life, to regard your foes with mercy and with love for their humanity—the ability to do these things is no mean accomplishment. If you constantly try to apply the principle of ikkyo to your life, your life will be filled with achievement and satisfaction. Ikkyo training is meant to teach you courage and pride under stress, to teach you to be peaceful in the face of aggression. Ikkyo is a state of mind as well as a technique. It gives you the power to influence others for their good, rather than to their detriment.

I once asked O Sensei what the true secret of Aikido was. He replied, "Ikkyo—that's it. I have taught it to you from the very beginning." It took me many years of study to realize the truth of his words. Now, as I watch my own students, I can understand O Sensei's frustration at my refusal to accept this point. Yet I also understand how difficult it is for people to believe that something so apparently simple is the hinge on which the door to understanding swings open.

Ikkyo is one movement. It is also the root of every movement in Aikido. It is the first movement and it is the last, the beginning and the end of technique. For if you can control the beginning of technique, do you not also control the end? It is the simplest of movements—just enter without fear. Yet behind this simple movement lies hundreds of years of battle, labor, practice, and mental and spiritual refinement. It is the principle that allows you to kill with one blow, yet it is the means by which you can stop conflict and demand peace. It is the beginning of your Aikido training, yet to fully comprehend its true meaning may take your whole life.

The Use of Weapons in Aikido

You may wonder, "Why train with swords or other old weapons if we are not studying sword technique, but principle? Why use archaic, outmoded weapons that are meaningless today?" True, we no longer fight with swords or jo or spears today. And it is also true that such weapons are useless against even a primitive gun well aimed, let alone the staggering array of exploding missiles in the world's arsenal today. And, yes, we are studying the principles and consciousness of budo, not sword kata for themselves.

Yet I think that work with weapons provides certain qualities in training that are difficult to discover with hand-to-hand technique. For one thing, weapons increase the intensity of your practice. It is much more painful and dangerous to be hit with a bokken or jo than an empty hand. It is possible to slip into egotistical toughness in empty hand practice. You may begin to be rougher on your partners than you should and become blind to the pain that you are causing them. When you are training with weapons, you become conscious very quickly that the consequences of careless, aggressive, or bullylike behavior can be disastrous. You become more aware of the possibility of pain and injury to both yourself and your partner. You become more concerned with defending yourself and with making sure that you do not hurt your partner. To see and feel another's pain and to extend compassion to your partner is an important step toward the development of ai nuke.

To avoid injury in weapons work you must learn concentration, alertness, precision, and decisiveness. All of these qualities are useful to develop both for your Aikido training and for your performance as a human being. Your sense of timing, of balance, of intuition, and of judgment all become more crucial in weapons work. You can't get away with the degree of sloppiness and inattention that you can sometimes overlook or be unaware of in hand-to-hand technique. You also develop more respect for your partners. If you are not respectful and attentive to them, they have the potential to do you a good deal of harm, even if it is unintentional.

Weapons are a wonderful equalizer. Say that you are a large, burly, strong man. That tiny woman that you so enjoyed hurling across the mat the other day may have you at a disadvantage with a bokken in her hands. Your superior weight, which you liked to impose on people in hand-to-hand technique, may slow you down, while she is quick and sharp in her movements. Your love affair with your muscular strength may have got in the way of your development of timing, precision, and intuition, whereas she, unable to depend on strength and size, has worked hard and honed her ability in all these things. Weapons have a way of teaching you humility and of making you aware of the deadly cost of a mistake.

Finally, the very archaic nature of the weapons we use in Aikido training has great value and has an important lesson to teach. A weapon like a sword or knife has a quality that is missing in modern weapons: it is personal. Today it is possible to send an airborne missile across the world and never have to see the bodies of its victims or the pain and injury that you have caused. You never have to look into the eyes of your victim. With a sword, you must confront your enemy face to face. The reality of the pain, of your opponent's existence as a living human being, is impossible to ignore.

Obviously, in a modern dojo, we do not kill, nor do we wish to. But the use of weapons, if you have any imagination at all, brings home to you the seriousness of your study and the terrible consequences of uncontrolled aggression. Weapons training should teach both compassion and restraint. Also, these older weapons leave you the power of choice from the beginning through the end of an encounter. If you fire a gun, you have made an irrevocable decision. You cannot stop the bullet in its deadly trajectory. A sword allows you the option of mercy. Once you have gained control, you can spare the enemy and give him the gift of his life. If you are aware of this aspect of the sword and the jo in your weapons training, it will help you learn to control your aggression. You will develop a more peaceful consciousness, where what you desire is not victory but an end to the struggle. In sum, weapons are a tool for training your spirit and refining your consciousness. As the weapon extends your physical reach, its use will extend you psychic grasp and will lend reality to the concepts you seek to grasp by studying Aikido.

Finally, let me leave you with these words that O Sensei spoke prior to performing a ritual dance with a bokken, on the symbolic importance of the sword. Keep his words in mind as you pursue your own training with weapons, and perhaps your sword will aid you also in connecting your consciousness to the universal truths.

Aikido trains the human spirit and invokes the great spirit of peace. Holding this bokken in my hands, I absorb the energy of the universe. I gather this ki unto myself and with my bokken cut through all evil. This is the divine technique of *misogi harai*. You must be able to show the light of love and wisdom on your surface, else you have not grasped the true spirit of bu. We must mirror the soul of the sword and rise to the divine state where we are at one with the eternal void. Such a consciousness is necessary in order to fulfill the mission of bu, of establishing peace throughout the world. We must stand at the center of the universe, free of the desire for competition or the need for victory. To be alive to the mystery of the threefold nature of the universe, to live at once in the physical, the astral, and the divine realms and yet remain conscious that it is one reality—this is the highest training of Aikido.

Since ancient times, three treasures have represented the spirit of Japan: the mirror, the sword, and the beads. They stand for wisdom, benevolence, and courage, the three great treasures within our hara, the depth of our being and consciousness, made real through actual training. This path, which makes its way through history, beginning with the divine age of the gods, will lead us to our own enlightenment, if we pay attention to its course. Awakening comes from deep within ourselves. Aikido gives us the ability to look into those depths and to ask where we came from and what should be our task. If we ask these questions correctly, we should surely find an answer. It is our responsibility to know ourselves, and self-knowledge is essential if we are to fulfill our divine mission. Humanity participates in the universal spirit, and each individual has an essential part to play in carrying out the divine plan of the universe. The bright and beautiful world is a manifestation of the workings of the divine harmony, and we are the recipients of its gift of life. The spiritual significance of the sword is to refrain from its use. Under the sign of the sword we must live in peace. We must purify ourselves. We must exorcise the darkness from our souls. We cannot spend our lives seeking pleasure or special favors. We must purge ourselves of anger, envy, and jealousy. We must not shrink from the challenges of life. We must not let these demons of our subconscious be reflected in the mirror of our actions in life. With courage in our hearts, we must take up the sword of judgment and create a harmonious society. This is the mission of the sword of the ancestor of mankind, the god Izanagi. This myth teaches us a lesson about the secret of bu.

The Aikido that I practice is a constructive path, it is for the creation of true human beings. It is not concerned with throwing people. It has no truck with self-indulgence. It is not for the purpose of taking life. It is the way of unifying the mind, body and spirit. All aikidoka must contemplate these truths with all seriousness of mind and heart.

Ichi-no-tachi shomenuchi ikkyo irimi. Shomenuchi ikkyo irimi is the same movement, whether performed with swords or with empty hands. In both cases the concern is with the first moment, the first contact. (*Ichi* means "one"; the word *ikkyo* derives from *ichi*.) Observe that the defender begins his movement simultaneously with the attacker; they move as one. The attacker's strike makes him open. The defender's response is both his first and his last, for with his first movement he takes control of the attacker's mind and body. The beginning is also the end. (Uke: Fernando Salazar and Patricia Saotome)

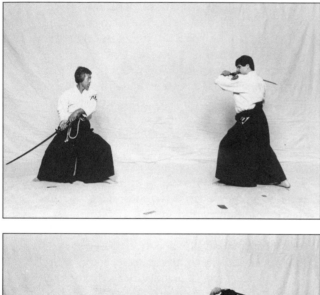

Kumiiai shomen ikkyo tenkan. A difference in timing causes the defender to take control of the attacker from the attacker's rear. However, the defender still controls the attacker's center from the beginning of the movement, commanding the progress of the technique from its inception. (Uke: Fernando Salazar)

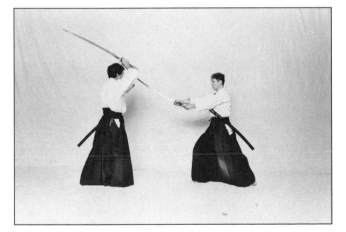

Kumitachi shomen ikkyo irimi. This version of shomenuchi ikkyo demonstrates the principle of *ude osai,* or control of uke's center through the arm. (Uke: Fernando Salazar)

Kumiiai shomen ikkyo. In this kumiiai version of ikkyo, the defender draws his sword simultaneously with the attacker's first strike. As the defender blocks the strike, he cuts down to the attacker's center, finishing the movement with a tsuki. Note the way he retreats at the end, lifting his sword in a block that covers his head and maintaining his focus on the attacker. This is an example of *zanshin,* the constant awareness of space and surroundings. Also, compare this version of ikkyo with others and note the differences in distance and timing that dictate nage's response to attack. The basic principles of ikkyo, however, remain the same in all examples. (Uke: Patricia Saotome)

Kumitachi

Kumiiai

Ikkyo with jo. This version of ikkyo with the jo is the equivalent of an empty hand tsuki ikkyo (not illustrated). The use of the jo demands that both hands operate in concert and that both sides of the body be balanced and aid each other. In empty hand techniques his bilateral balance is just as important but is easier to forget. If you compare this series of photographs with those of empty hand ikkyo techniques, you will notice that the arm movement that the defender uses to accomplish both is identical. (Uke: Patricia Saotome)

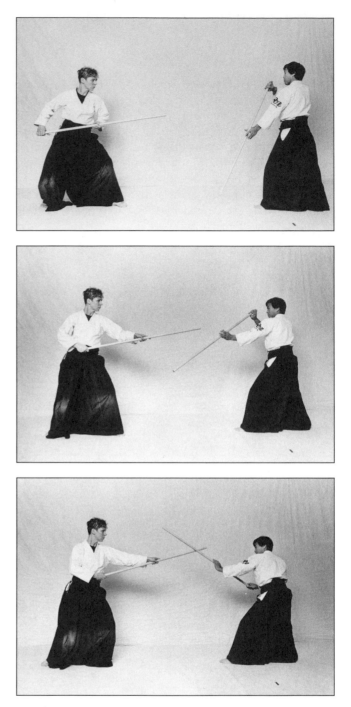

Ikkyo Kumijo. This is the first kata in a series of six basic jo kata. The initial attack and block are equivalent to empty hand tsuki ikkyo (not illustrated). The use of weapons extends, elongates, and enlarges reach and movement and allows the student to gain a clearer understanding of the correct execution of movement. Weapons work also forces the student to be more alert and careful in practice, as the consequences of laxity are potentially dangerous to both defender and attacker. Jo work also emphasizes smoothness and fluidity of movement, as both ends of the jo are used to block, strike, and thrust and the jo is often rotated in the course of a kata. (Uke: Patricia Saotome)

Jo ikkyo from empty hand grab. This technique is initiated by nage thrusting at uke with his jo. Uke grabs the jo to defend herself against the tsuki. Nage uses uke's hold on the jo to accomplish an ikkyo on uke. Using the jo magnifies the movements involved in the technique. One sees clearly the spirals, control of the center, and ude osai that characterize ikkyo. (Uke: Patricia Saotome)

Jo ikkyo from empty hand shomen and tsuki. These two series provide further evidence of the parallel between empty hand and weapons techniques. If you study these series and compare them with other ikkyo series, both armed and empty-handed, you should be able to see the similarity of movements. Practice where one partner is armed and the other is not furnish a good link between empty hand and weapons technique. (Uke: Patricia Saotome)

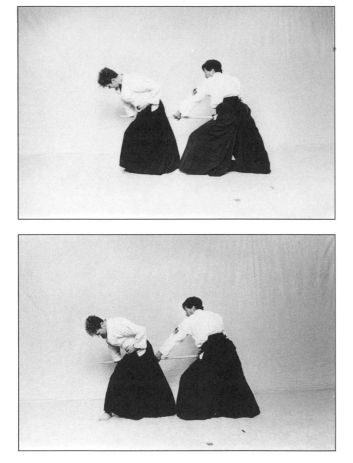

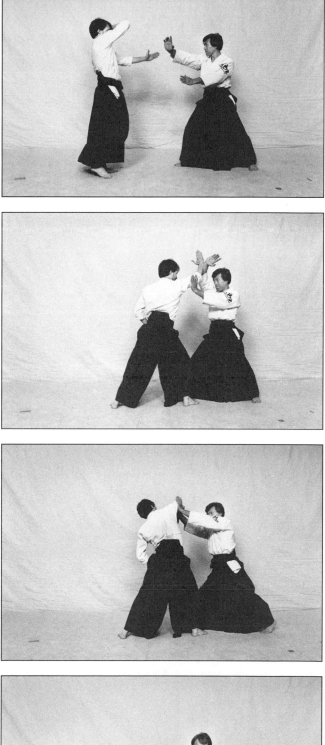

Shomenuchi ikkyo irimi. Note how nage, in executing ikkyo, moves to cover and control uke's center from the beginning of the technique. Nage takes over the opening that uke makes in raising his arm to strike. When you compare this empty hand version of shomenuchi ikkyo to that performed with swords, take care to observe that the hand motion of nage as he begins his movement is exactly the same as that which he uses in raising his sword to tsuki. (Uke: Don Moock)

46

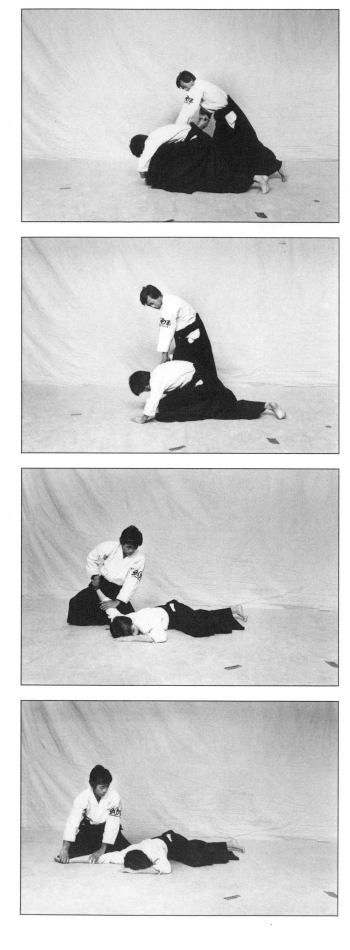

Shomenuchi ikkyo tenkan. A subtle adjustment of timing and distance dictates the difference between ikkyo irimi and ikkyo tenkan. Here nage takes the opening that uke offers and moves off the line of uke's attack slightly to uke's back. Nage takes uke's balance by stepping behind him. This technique offers a clear example of ude osai, or control of uke's center through uke's arm. (Uke: Don Moock)

48

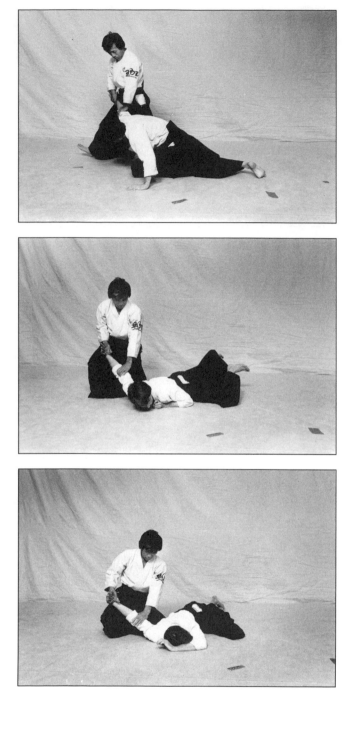

Shomenuchi ikkyo (detail). The execution of ikkyo depends on nage's direct penetration to uke's center. Observe how nage blocks uke's arm and uses atemi to counter uke's strike. Not until close to the end of the technique does nage actually grasp uke's arm. This series of photographs illustrates the principle that defense and offense are inseparable. (Uke: Wendy Whited)

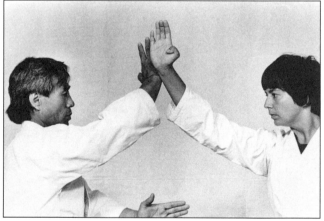

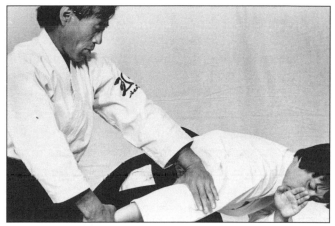

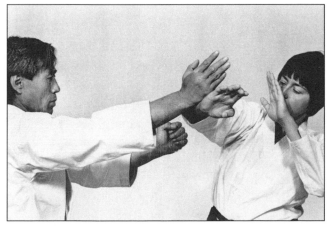

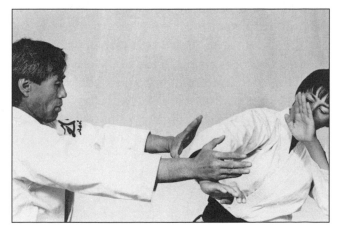

6

Techniques from Shomenuchi

Shomenuchi, or a blow to the front of the head with the blade of the hand, derives from sword technique, as do many elements of Aikido. This is one of the reasons that it is important to pay close attention to the relationship between empty hand and weapons techniques in Aikido. Aikido is descended from the arts that the samurai learned in order to be able to continue fighting armed opponents should they be so unfortunate as to lose or break their weapons in battle. It is important to bear this in mind in your training. Sometimes people forget, because of the emphasis on the spiritual in Aikido, that its techniques are based on self-defense in life-and-death situations. This is not an art to train street fighters. It is an art that teaches complete consciousness of your openings and vulnerabilities. This is another reason that physical strength and competition are meaningless in Aikido. A blow that is harmless or at most uncomfortable if your opponent is unarmed can be fatal if a weapon is being used. You should practice every technique with this in mind. Shomenuchi is not a particularly effective way to hurt someone with an empty hand, but if you consider the effect of the same type of blow with a sword, you will see the grisly picture of yourself cloven in half. You should try to respond to each attack in practice as if your opponent were armed. If you lose this consciousness, your perception will become clouded. You will lose the ability to learn where you are truly vulnerable, and will struggle uselessly to execute or to resist technique when you have already, in essence, been killed.

Yes, Aikido practice is gentle, but behind that gentleness is a terrible severity—the question of life and death. Toughness and brutality have no meaning in the face of such a question. This is the reason that humility in your training is not just a nicety of practice; it is essential. You and your partners hold each other's lives in trust.

Atemi Points for Shomenuchi

Atemi and direct strikes are not often used in response to attack in Aikido training, yet they play an important role in the development of nage's perception. If nage is not within distance to deliver an effective strike, he will not be within distance to execute effective technique. Also, the use of atemi teaches both nage and uke to be aware of the openings that an attack creates. If nage knows where uke is vulnerable, nage will be aware of what the defensive options are. If nage knows what the choices are in responding to uke's attack, nage will not become obsessed with the failure or success of one particular technique and will have the freedom to choose the more benevolent method of controlling uke. If unaware of uke's openings and the options they present, nage is more likely to be insecure and aggressive; atemiwaza are useful for reinforcing the awareness of the life-and-death potential of techniques.

To refrain from destructive behavior, you must know what possibilities of both destruction and protection are open to you. You cannot make an educated choice if you do not know what your choices are. The series of photographs that follow depict some of the openings for atemi that the shomenuchi attack presents. When viewing these techniques, remember that every attack presents its own openings and weak points. Keep this in mind when viewing attacks for which no atemiwaza are shown.

Shomenuchi iriminage in the Sarasota dojo
(Uke: Hiroshi Ikeda; photograph by P. Saotome)

Seiza and Suwariwaza

All martial arts have their specialties and distinguishing features. One of Aikido's specialties is suwariwaza, or techniques from a seated position called seiza, in which you sit with your knees folded under you. Some of these techniques are performed with nage and uke virtually stationary, like kokyu tanden ho. Others employ shikko, or the traditional Japanese method of knee walking.

The presence of suwariwaza in Aikido is rooted in tradition and history, and it is further evidence of Aikido's origin in the martial arts of the samurai. Seiza and shikko were very much a part of the samurai life-style. The higher class Japanese households tended to cover their floors with tatami mats and they used little furniture. The people in the household sat on the floor either in seiza or crosslegged. They often moved from place to place using shikko, rather than rising to their feet, walking upright and sitting back down again. Because much of their time indoors was spent sitting in seiza, the samurai had to learn to defend themselves from that position. The suwariwaza techniques of Aikido evolved from the samurai's necessity.

Today, we do not have the same need to defend ourselves against hostile swordbearing gentlemen who have come into our house in the guise of guests. "Why not do away with suwariwaza techniques?" some will ask. "They are obsolete and very uncomfortable and difficult to perform." So they are, but they have great physical benefits for the student of Aikido if practiced diligently. Suwariwaza will make your feet and legs strong and flexible. Because you are moving so close to the ground, you will gain an increased connection with gravity and a deeper sense of stability. Suwariwaza will improve your sense of center and therefore your balance. Because the mobility of your legs is much more restricted in suwariwaza than in standing techniques, suwariwaza forces you to improve the relaxation and flexibility of your upper body. It is also very difficult to walk in shikko if your upper body is stiff. If you become comfortable and effective in suwariwaza, it will improve your standing techniques. You will find that the strength, flexibility, and increase in centeredness that you gain is worth the effort of practicing suwariwaza.

More about Shomenuchi

After the beginner in Aikido is ready to deal with striking attacks, shomenuchi is perhaps most commonly used. One reason is that it is both very threatening and very safe. People naturally are more frightened of blows to the head and face than of any other type of blow. Shomenuchi invokes that fear, and yet its target in practice, the front of the forehead, is one of the most invulnerable points in the human anatomy. The danger of injury to the student who misses the technique and gets hit is almost nil.

Shomenuchi, then, serves a double purpose. It reinforces the consciousness that every technique should be practiced as if life and death were at stake because it forces the student to confront fear. Yet as the student learns that he or she will at most suffer a little pain if hit by a shomenuchi, the student will learn to come to terms with fear and reduce it. The student

will begin to absorb the principle of irimi—enter without fear. Here we see again the principle of yin and yang in Aikido. You must practice as if your life were at stake in each encounter, yet you must learn to face each encounter without fear. Shomenuchi training helps in the development of such a consciousness. You know that you cannot be hurt by the empty hand shomenuchi, so you lose the habit of fear. Yet in your imagination, the upraised sword is held in the hand, and you hone your response to the attack to defend against its deadly threat. Both reactions should grow side by side.

Keep these ideas in mind as you study the techniques from shomenuchi.

Shomenuchi ikkyo with elbow break. The original purpose of the arm control shown in this version of ikkyo was not just to throw uke but to crush or break the elbow joint. It is important to be aware of the original purposes of Aikido techniques in your practice and to know where you are vulnerable. This technique demonstrates concretely why resistance to nage's throws can be not only counterproductive, but dangerous and foolish, if you do not know the purpose and the possibilities of a technique. (Uke: Fernando Salazar)

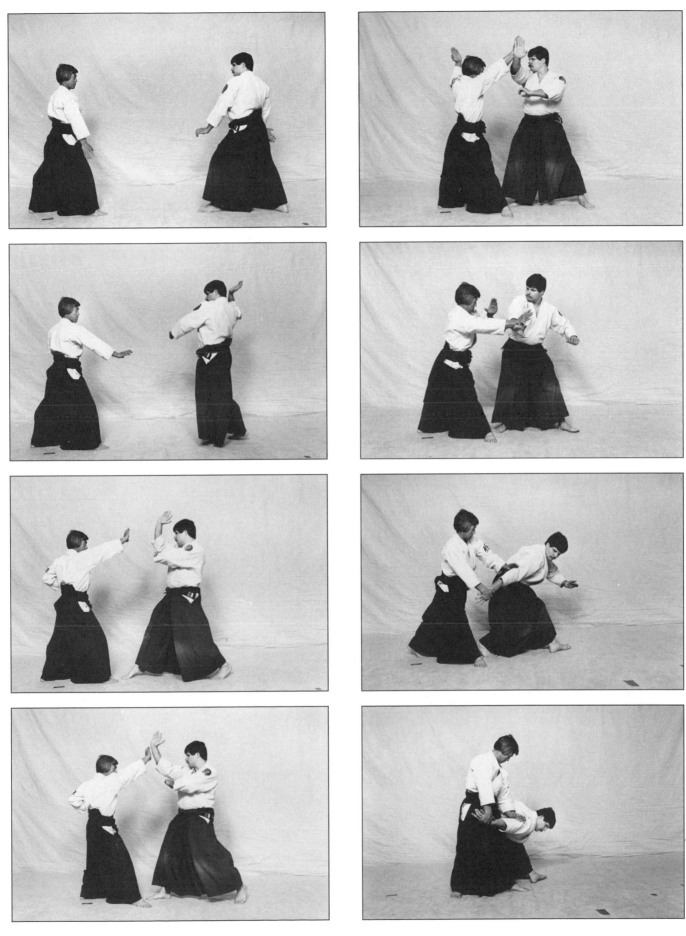

Shomenuchi irimi with atemi to the jaw. As uke attacks, nage makes an irimi movement in response and delivers an atemi to the vulnerable and open point under uke's arm. His other hand, which has retracted with his irimi movement then uncoils for a strike to uke's jaw. This type of practice should be done slowly, as it can be dangerous. Note that nage uses an open hand to push uke's jaw, rather than using a fist. The safety and well-being of one's partner cannot be neglected when you are practicing atemiwaza. (Uke: Don Moock)

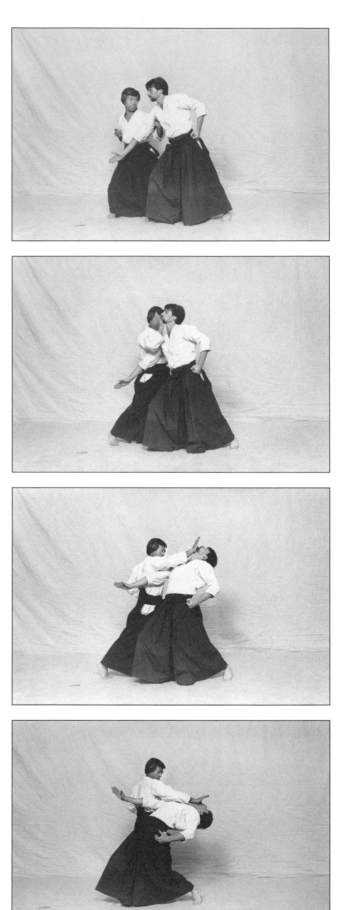

Shomenuchi iriminage. The iriminage depicted here is a more benign version of the previous technique. The movements of nage are exactly the same, but here nage chooses to block uke's attack and throw him, rather than use the double atemi shown in the previous series. Nage's knowledge of the possibility of using atemi, however, is what enables him to execute this iriminage successfully. (Uke: Don Moock)

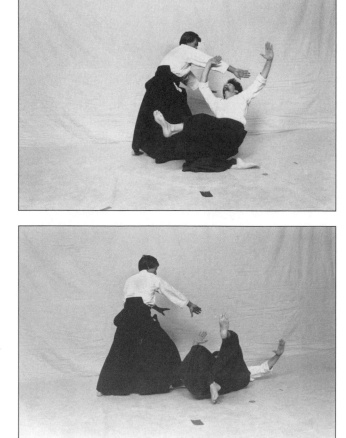

Shomenuchi irimi with atemi to the throat, and with atemi to the solar plexus. The shomenuchi attack leaves uke vulnerable in many points along his center line. In the movements depicted in these two series of photographs nage enters directly to uke's center and delivers strikes to uke's throat (in the first series) and solar plexus (in the second). Nage's movement in both techniques is the same, and the difference exists solely in the vulnerable point on uke that nage chooses to attack. An acute sense of timing and distance are essential to the successful execution of this type of irimi, whether atemi are employed or not. A half-inch constitutes the difference between safety and defeat for nage. Note that nage's footwork consists mainly in changing hanmi. Nage does not attempt to escape but enters directly to uke's center. This encounter between uke and nage has the initial appearance of ai uchi but resolves into ai nuke, as nage controls the situation and asserts—but does not take advantage of—his possession of uke's life. (Uke: Fernando Salazar)

Shomenuchi irimi ikkyo with atemi to the side. Here you may observe one of the options available to nage among the infinite possibilities of ikkyo. After blocking uke's strike, nage uses an atemi to uke's side, rather than controlling uke's elbow. When executing a conventional ikkyo, you must be aware of the openings and the possibilities for atemi. If you are not in a position to deliver the atemi, you are not in a position to execute ikkyo. (Uke: Fernando Salazar)

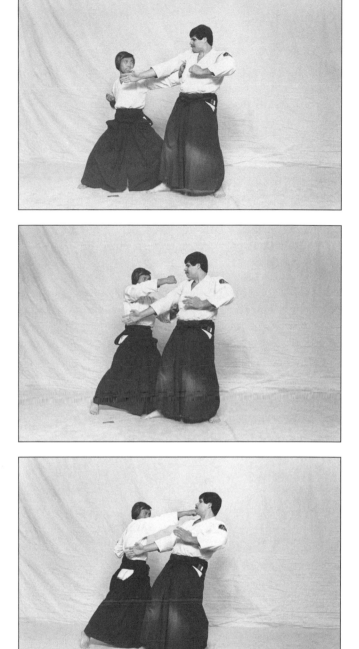

Shomenuchi irimi with atemi to the jaw. This series of photographs, showing the shomenuchi attack, with nage responding with the same combination of atemi to the underarm and then to the jaw shown earlier, displays an additional important point. Note that nage uses his hand to distract and occupy uke's vision until he is ready to enter for the atemi to uke's side. This allows nage to control the timing of the encounter between himself and uke, and gives him the freedom to execute a successful irimi. (Uke: Fernando Salazar)

Tachidori ikkyo suwariwaza. Among the many martial arts that Morihei Ueshiba O Sensei studied in his journey toward creating Aikido was Shin Kage ryu tachidori, the art of taking a sword away from an enemy when one is unarmed. Here the disarming of uke through ikkyo is begun in seiza and completed in shikko. Tachidori (sword taking) dramatically illustrates the truth that there is no difference between empty hand and weapons techniques. The unarmed defender is equal to the armed attacker *if* the guiding principles of Aikido are followed. In this series one can observe the lack of separation between attack and response, the control of uke's center by nage from the first moment, and the advantage that nage takes of the opening that uke's attack creates. Once nage is in control of uke's center, the sword ceases to be of any use to her. It is important to remember that the sword itself is not the enemy but the person who wields it. In tachidori techniques you must not become distracted by or obsessed with the weapon. (Uke: Patricia Saotome)

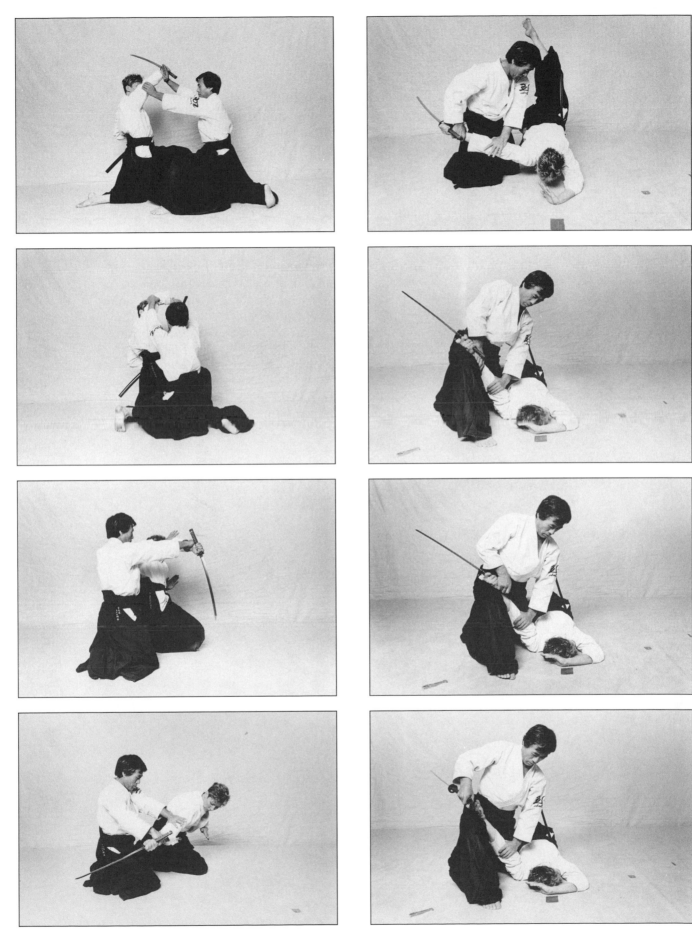

62

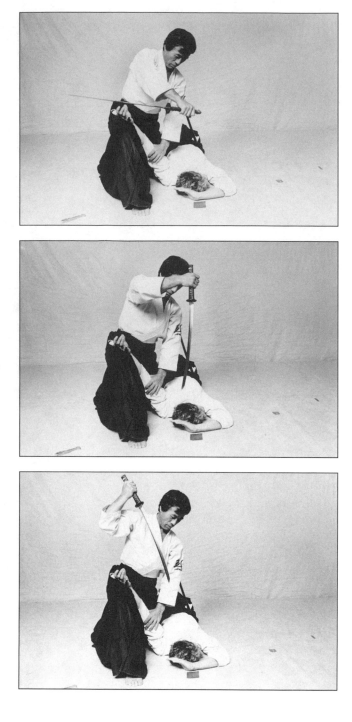

Suwariwaza shomenuchi ikkyo omote. The terms *omote* and *ura* relate to irimi and tenkan, respectively, but are not the same. *Irimi* and *tenkan* refer to movement principles; *omote* and *ura* refer to physical position. Omote means that nage is in front of uke's face; ura means that nage is behind uke. Ura generally employs centrifugal power, while omote employs centripetal power. In this ikkyo omote you can see that nage moves into the front of uke's body. As he meets uke's attack, nage moves his center along with his arm. You will note that all through this technique nage keeps his body unified and balanced. His legs remain underneath him and his arms are never overextended. They are always connected to his hips and center. Also observe here that nage's execution of ikkyo involves not grabbing and wrestling with uke's arm but using uke's arm to push through his center and then extend him outward. (Uke: Chuck Weber)

Suwariwaza shomenuchi ikkyo ura. The successful execution of ikkyo is as much dependent on nage maintaining the correct mental attitude as on physical technique. The physical limitations of suwariwaza help to make the mind more free. Because his body is not as mobile, nage's consciousness must become more supple. This series of photographs also provides a clear view of the spinning centrifugal power of the ura, or tenkan, movement and of nage's position behind uke. (Uke: Chuck Weber)

Shomenuchi iriminage. This technique provides an excellent illustration of how the symbiosis between uke and nage works in Aikido technique. After nage enters behind uke with an irimi movement, he breaks uke's balance with a tenkan movement. Uke attempts to catch up to nage's movement and to rise and regain his balance. As uke begins to stand erect, he creates the opportunity for nage to make the throw. Nage and uke both reflect and work off of each other's movement. Uke does not resist the force of nage's tenkan movement but rather protects himself by following nage, an action that also keeps open his opportunities to reverse the technique (kaeshiwaza) and regain his advantage. Nage does not drag uke down and then haul him back up again for the throw but rather uses the breaking of uke's balance and uke's subsequent attempt to regain it to bring uke into position for the throw. It is fairly evident even in still photographs that timing and correct position, not brute strength, create the moment of the throw. Compare this technique with the following suwariwaza iriminage tachidori. (Uke: Don Moock)

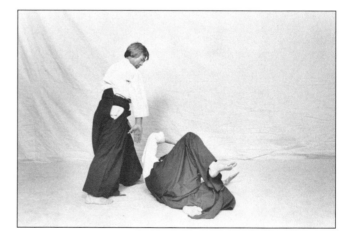

Suwariwaza iriminage tachidori. This is the equivalent of the empty hand technique, suwariwaza shomenuchi iriminage (not illustrated). Note the close resemblance of nage's initial movement to that used in shomenuchi ikkyo. (Uke: Patricia Saotome)

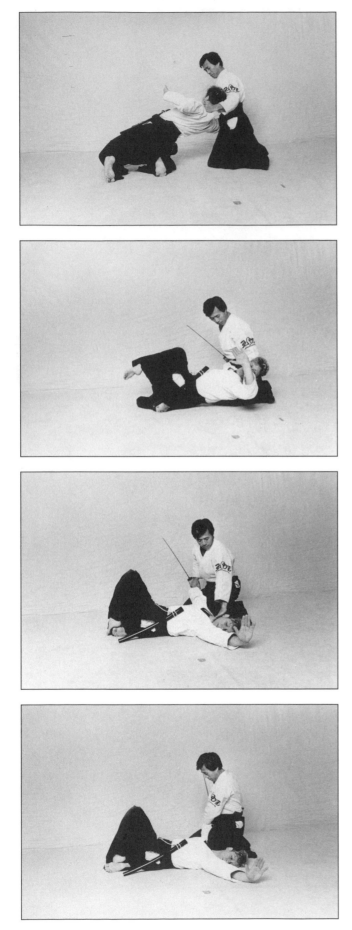

Shomenuchi nikyo ura. Communication and cooperation between uke and nage in Aikido practice help make for good training. Cooperation, in Aikido, does not mean that uke automatically acquiesces to any action that nage takes. Rather, it means that uke must be aware of the conditions that he or she is trying to create for nage so that nage may practice a particular technique. Uke must also respond appropriately to nage's movements. Nage must be aware that uke is giving him or herself willingly to nage for the purposes of training. While making use of the training opportunity that uke is giving, nage must never take unfair advantage of uke's cooperation. The technique shown here, shomenuchi nikyo ura, provides a good example of what is meant by cooperation between uke and nage. Nage, when executing nikyo, should always begin by sincerely trying for ikkyo. Uke in turn resists the ikkyo and his resistance creates an appropriate occasion for nage to perform nikyo. See how uke rises after nage has performed the ikkyo ura movement, attempting to regain his balance and break free of nage's control. At this point nage applies nikyo, which flows naturally as a continuation of the ikkyo and reasserts nage's control of the technique. You may observe two important points about nikyo in this series. First, note that nage keeps control of uke's body through his hold on uke's elbow; the rotation of uke's arm connects the arm with his shoulder and center. If nage lost control of uke, he would not be able to transform his ikkyo into nikyo. Second, as nage applies the nikyo, you can see that his attention is focused on uke's entire person, not just his hand. Nage should keep the hand he has at uke's elbow free enough to guard against, or to deliver, a strike if the need should arise. (Uke: Don Moock)

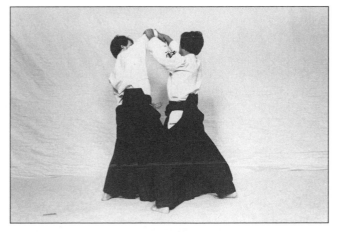

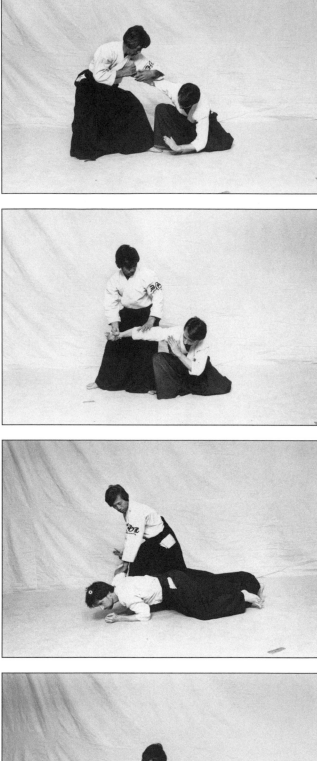

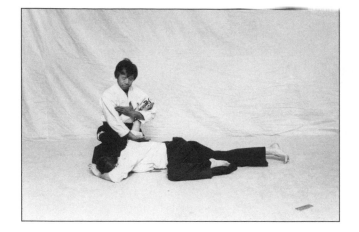

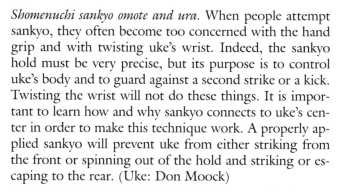

Shomenuchi sankyo omote and ura. When people attempt sankyo, they often become too concerned with the hand grip and with twisting uke's wrist. Indeed, the sankyo hold must be very precise, but its purpose is to control uke's body and to guard against a second strike or a kick. Twisting the wrist will not do these things. It is important to learn how and why sankyo connects to uke's center in order to make this technique work. A properly applied sankyo will prevent uke from either striking from the front or spinning out of the hold and striking or escaping to the rear. (Uke: Don Moock)

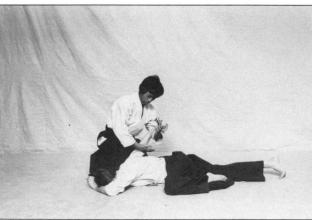

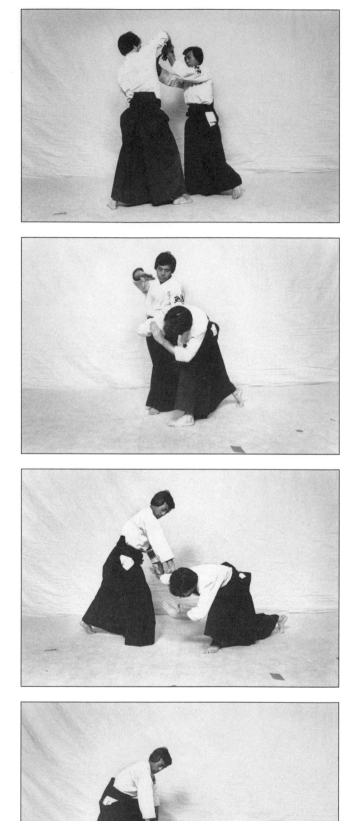

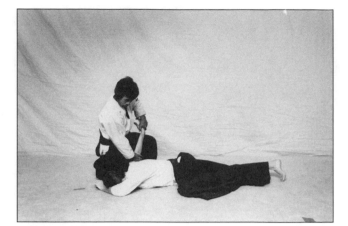

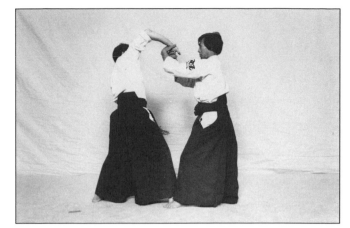

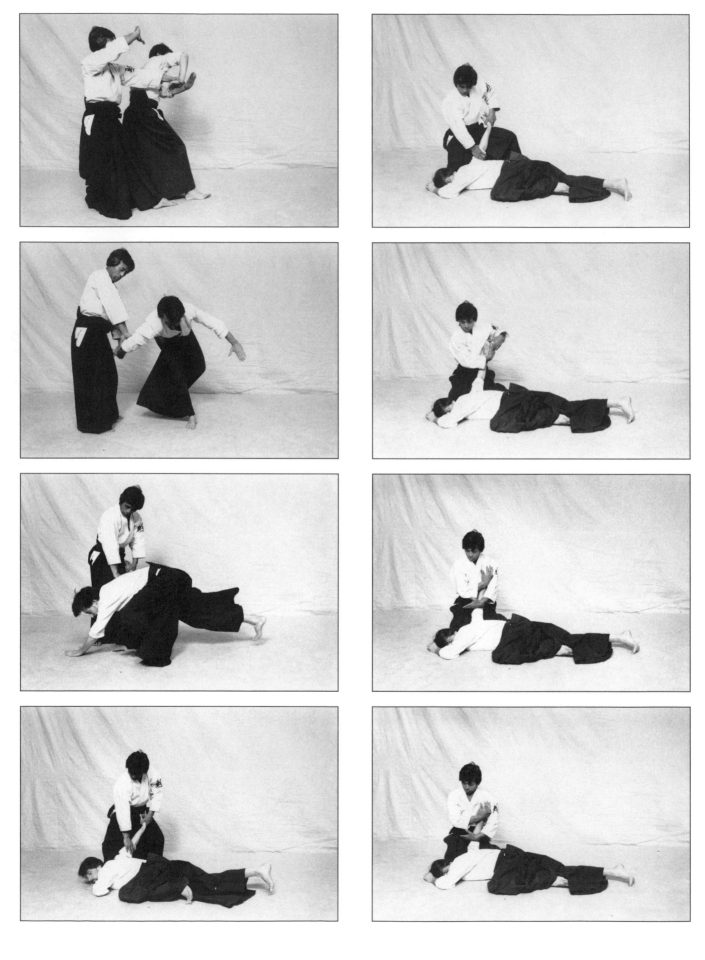

Shomenuchi yonkyo omote. Yonkyo is a particularly difficult technique. While yonkyo does involve pressing a nerve in the forearm against the radial bone, its success, like that of sankyo, is dependent on the control of uke's whole body, not on the infliction of pain. Many students forget this point and just try to go for the pain. However, students' pain tolerance will increase as they practice and pressure on the nerve won't work on most advanced students. Instead of concentrating on finding the nerve center, it is better to learn to make your hold on the forearm connect to uke's center of balance, through the elbow and shoulder. Here nage performs a seated pin at the finish. (Uke: Don Moock)

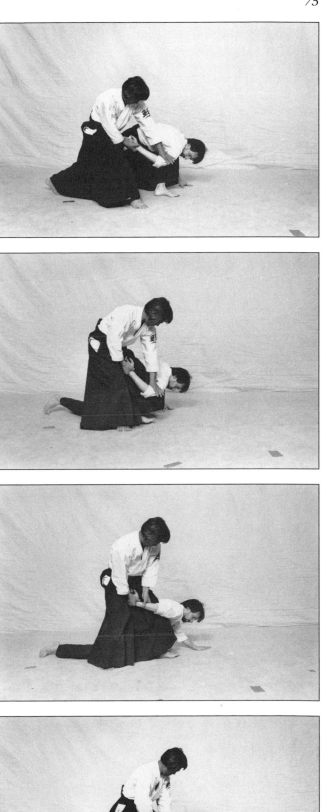

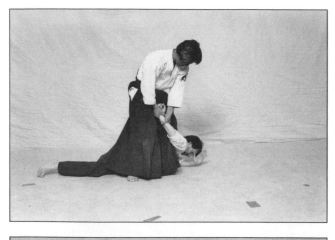

Shomenuchi yonkyo ura. The movement for yonkyo is like that for cutting with a sword. While true of both the omote and ura versions, it is easier to see in the ura. Nage holds uke's forearm in a two-handed grip as he would a sword. He raises uke's arm and cuts down with it across his own front, as when performing kesa giri. At the end of the cut, nage's arms extend and his hands tighten together in front of him, the way a good sword cut should finish. The yonkyo hold must be precise, and nage must use it to guard against the chance of uke spinning out of the hold to the rear or striking with his other hand. Nage ends with a standing pin. His knee is tightly pressed into the inside of uke's elbow to control uke's shoulder and body. (Uke: Don Moock)

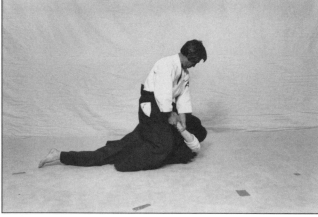

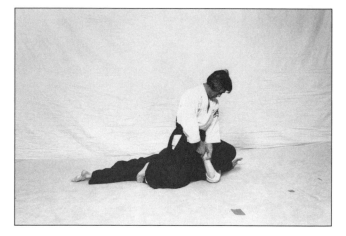

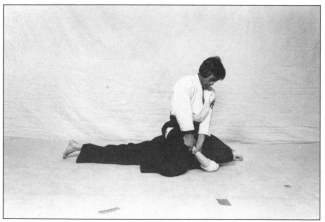

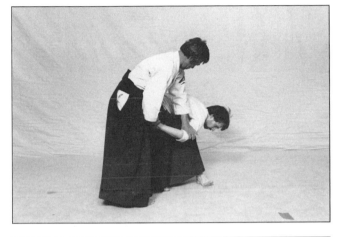

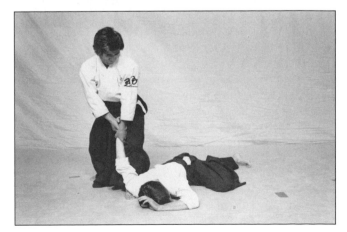

7
Techniques from Yokomenuchi

Yokomenuchi is a blow with the blade of the hand to the side of the head or the neck. This attack is derived from the sword attack kesa giri, which is a diagonal cut across the body, starting at the neck. Yokomenuchi attacks provide good training in forcing nage to concentrate on uke's center, rather than allowing his attention to be drawn away to the side by the striking hand. The reader will note that the majority of sword techniques paired with comparable empty hand techniques are in this section.

Yokomenuchi ikkyo omote and ura. Yokomenuchi ikkyo provides a good illustration of the principle of musubi in action. Nage absorbs uke's strike with his arms and body movement, rather than blocking and stopping uke. He uses uke's momentum to draw uke off balance and downward. When nage releases pressure on uke's arm, uke naturally attempts to stand up and regain his balance. Nage takes advantage of the opening that this gives him to complete the ikkyo. Note that nage commands uke's center from the beginning of the movement, as should always be the case in ikkyo. In the tenkan version of this technique, observe the circular movements typical of aikido technique. From the start of the technique nage forms the axis, and uke forms the periphery, of the movement. (Uke: Don Moock)

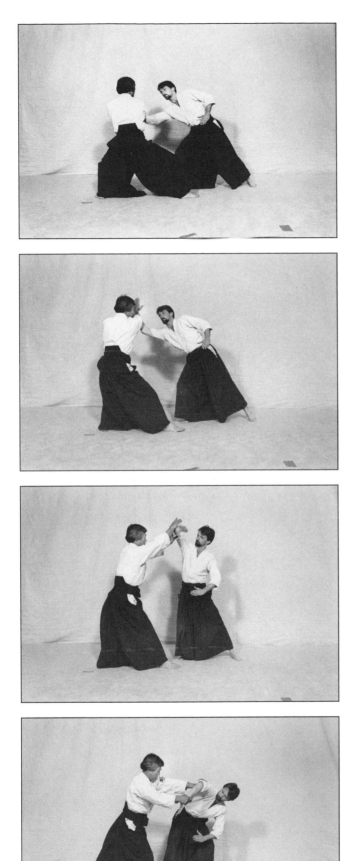

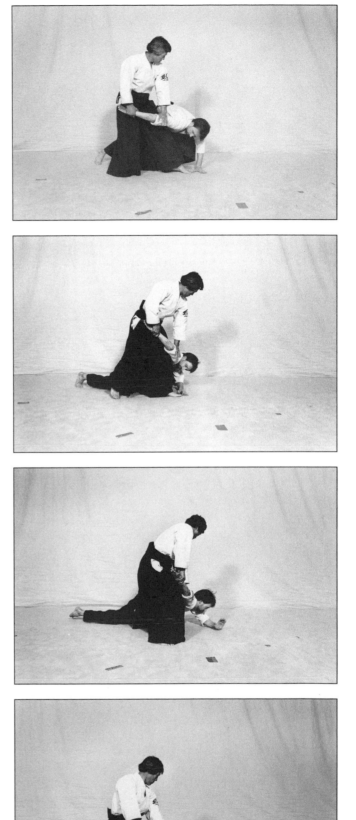

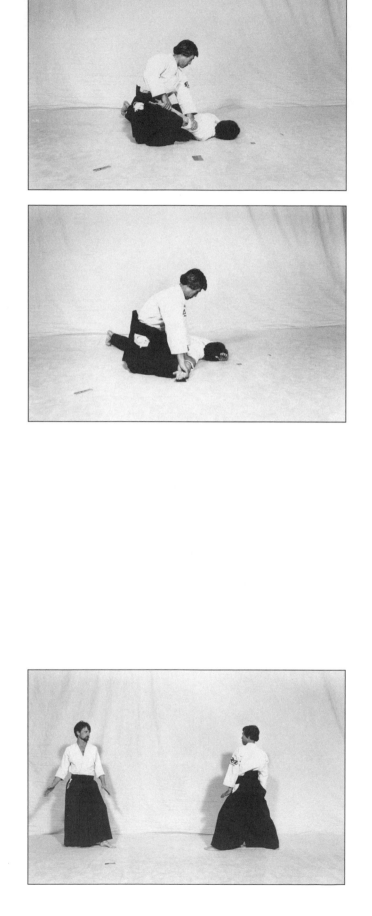

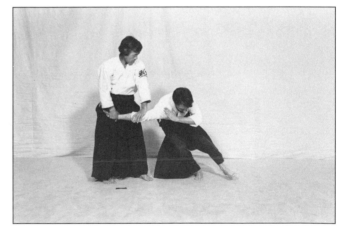

82

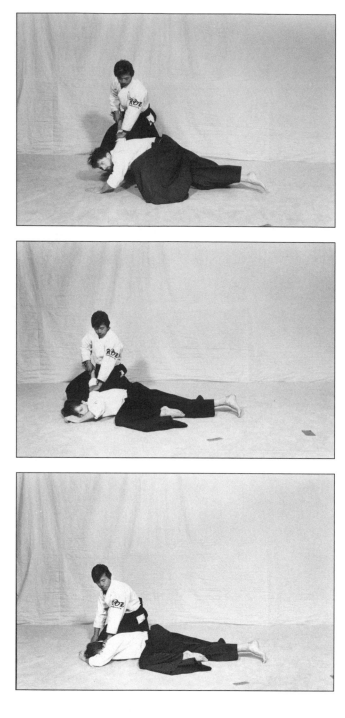

Yokomenuchi block (detail). This type of yokomenuchi block is frequently used to begin yokomenuchi ikkyo techniques. As always, nage covers uke's center. Note the spiral motion of nage's blocking hand at the end. This ensures that nage's block and cut will be continuous and that he will not lose contact with uke. (Uke: Don Moock)

Kumitachi yokomen ikkyo irimi. The principle behind this kumitachi is that of inazuma (lightning). Inazuma refers to the zigzag shape drawn by the block and the kote giri (wrist cut) performed by the defender. This type of block-and-cut pattern is also referred to as ku no ji giri, or a cut in the shape of the character *ku*, which also has a jagged shape. Compare this kumitachi with empty hand yokomenuchi ikkyo; the block and cut have the same shape in both techniques. Also, both empty hand and kumitachi versions of this technique use the rebound of the impact of the block to create the opening for the cut. You must use the rhythm of uke's response to the block in both. (Uke: Fernando Salazar)

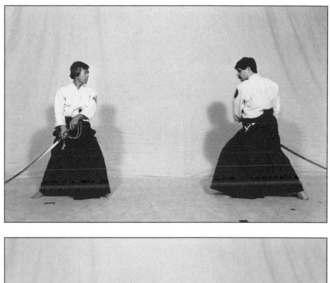

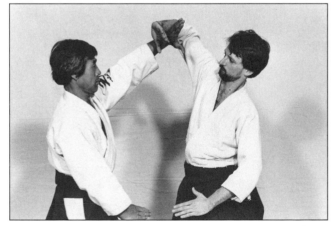

85

Kumitachi yokomen yokomen ikkyo. This kumitachi relates to yokomenuchi ikkyo omote. If you compare this technique with the empty hand version, you will be able to see that nage's movements are the same in both. (Uke: Fernando Salazar)

Kumitachi yokomen yokomen ikkyo. In ikkyo, attack and defense are one; movement and response form an inseparable unit. Notice how all through this series nage's movements are a reflection of uke's and vice-versa. It is nage's alterations in timing and position that allow him to maintain and finish the technique in his position of advantage. Compare this to empty hand yokomenuchi ikkyo. (Uke: Fernando Salazar)

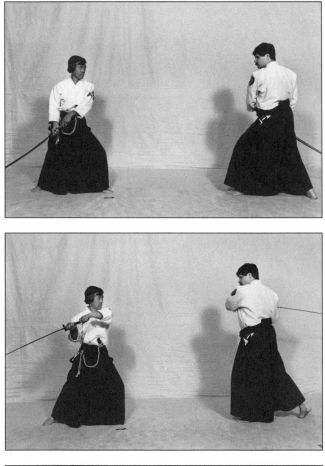

Yokomenuchi irimi with atemi. In responding to any attack, the Aikido student must overcome the tendency to focus on the striking or grabbing hand to the exclusion of the rest of uke's body. This tendency seems to be particularly strong with yokomenuchi attacks, since these attacks are to the side of the head or neck. The temptation to turn away from uke's center is therefore greater. In this version of yokomenuchi irimi, nage does not block uke's yokomen at all but moves directly into uke's center with an atemi. Timing and confidence are necessary to the successful execution of this technique. Nage must move quickly and straight in, without hesitating. Note also how nage guards his center and occupies uke's vision with his upraised hand at the inception of this technique. When nage moves in with the atemi, he changes hanmi. At no point does he take his focus off uke's center, nor does he leave his own center uncovered. (Uke: Don Moock)

Kumitachi yokomen tsuki irimi. This kumitachi illustrates the importance of the defender controlling and covering the attacker's center rather than focusing on the attack. Notice that the defender does not block the attacker's yokomen but strikes straight to the attacker's center, which has been left vulnerable by the attack. Compare this technique with the previously shown empty hand yokomenuchi irimi. (Uke: Fernando Salazar)

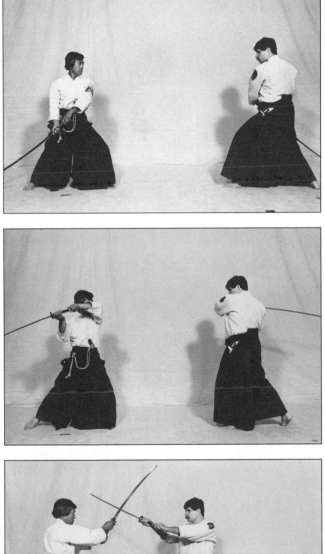

Yokomenuchi nikyo omote. This version of yokomenuchi nikyo uses an irimi entry. Nage moves directly into the strike, blocking it before it has developed full strength. Thus he draws uke off balance by catching the attack at its weak point, rather than forcing uke to overextend his strike. Notice that nage moves his whole body off the line. He does not stand in front of uke, leaving himself vulnerable to a second attack. At the same time that he blocks, nage delivers an atemi to uke's solar plexus. This atemi naturally continues into the cut under uke's striking arm that begins the nikyo. (Uke: Don Moock)

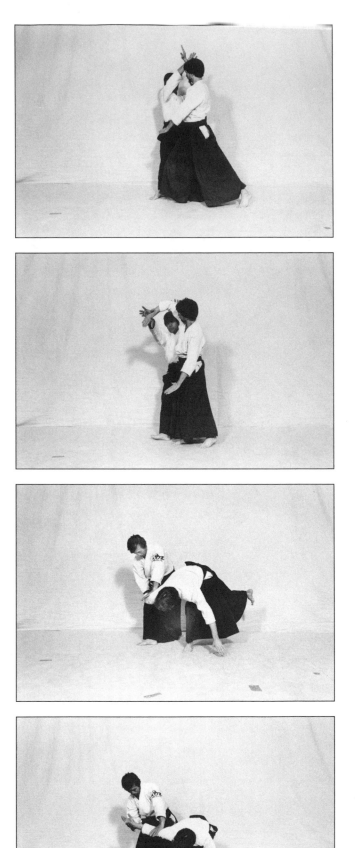

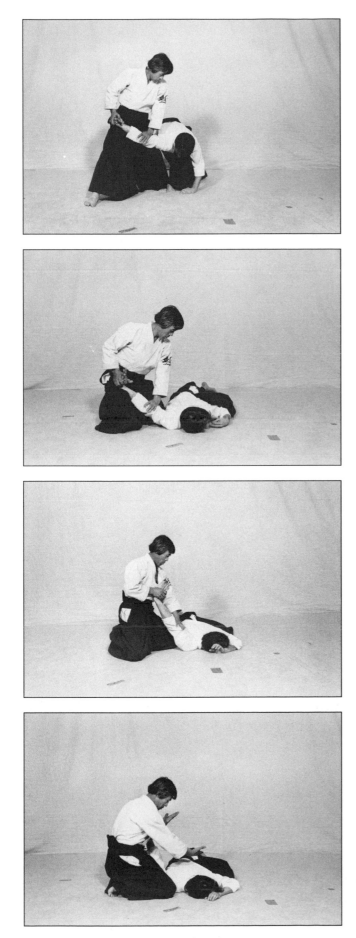

Yokomenuchi nikyo ura. Once again, it is important here that nage keeps his hold on uke's elbow. Otherwise nage could not execute this technique. Note how nage brings uke's hand up to his shoulder and uses the pressure of his whole body to apply the nikyo. This use of the shoulder makes for a more effective connection to uke's center. This technique is very difficult to do if you just use arm strength. The same is true for the final pin. Nage uses his whole body to twist uke's arm. (Uke: Don Moock)

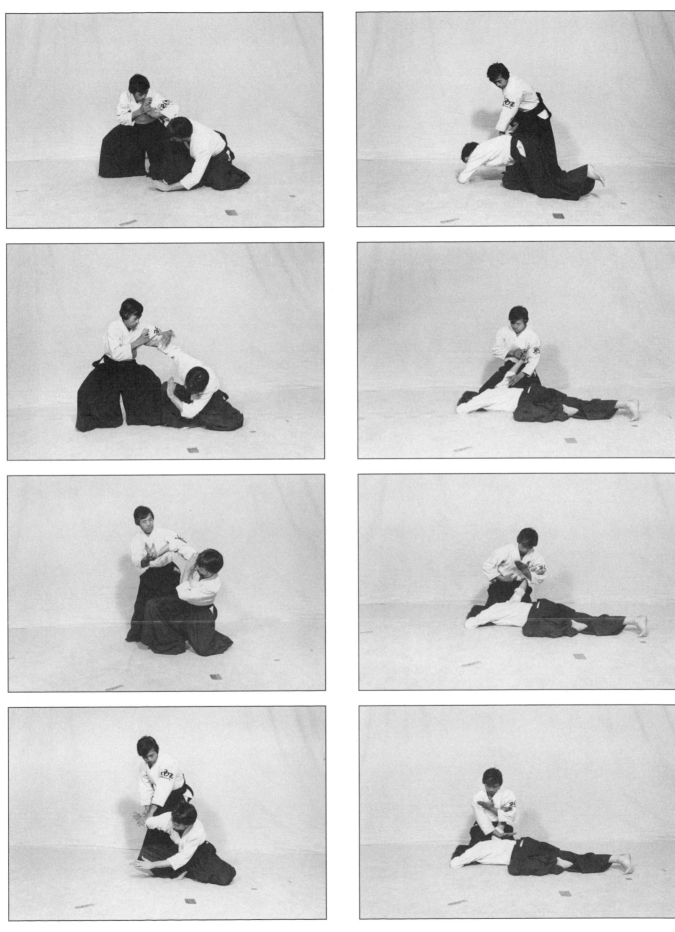

Yokomenuchi sankyo omote. In this technique, note how nage uses his leg and hip to control uke's body. Without this type of control, uke can often walk away from the technique. This is a good point to keep in mind when studying any ikkyo-based technique. Observe also how nage's control of uke's wrist extends through uke's whole body. (Uke: Don Moock)

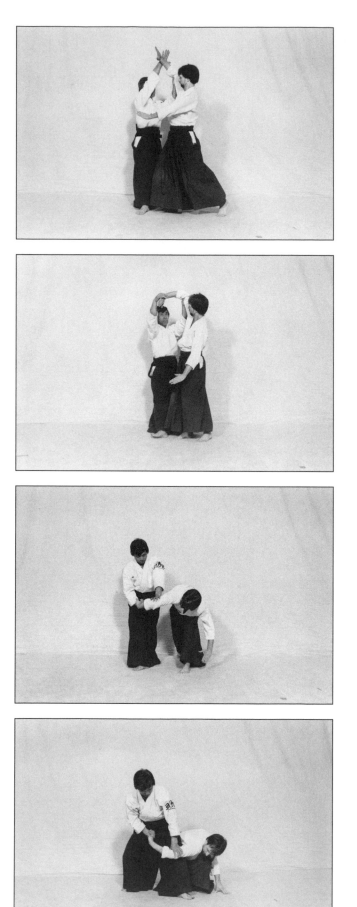

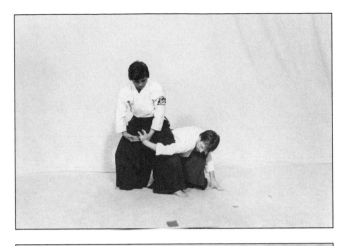

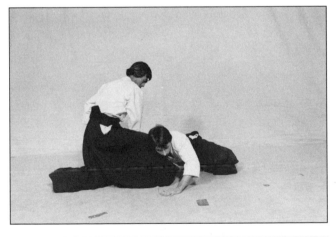

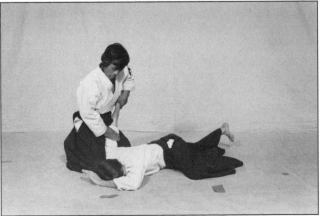

Yokomenuchi sankyo ura. Most people naturally will try to resist physical constraint. Many Aikido techniques take advantage of this instinctive resistance. Here, for instance, uke pushes back against the sankyo. Nage allows uke to go in the direction he desires but guides his arm downward and behind him to complete the technique. It is a redirection of uke's own movement—not coercion by nage—that makes this technique work. (Uke: Don Moock)

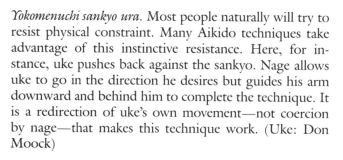

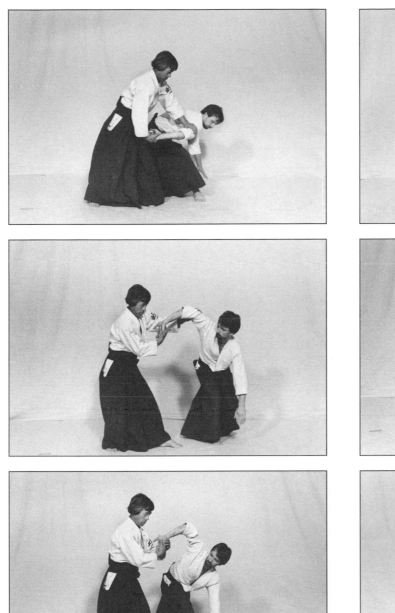

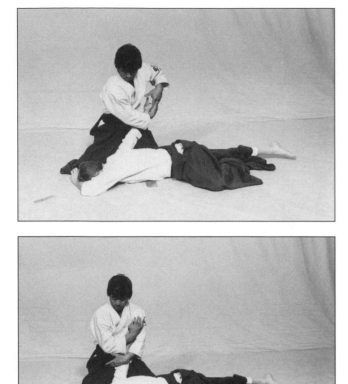

Kumitachi yokomen yokomen sankyo (two views). This technique should be examined and compared with empty hand yokomenuchi sankyo. The sequence of cuts and blocks that make up this sword technique are parallel to that movement, and they also help clarify the reasons for both uke's and nage's responses in the progress of this technique. The pressure of the defender's initial block and its subsequent release prompts the attacker's attempts to bring his sword around for a second yokomen to the defender's other side. This parallels uke's attempt to retract his hand and regain his balance in the empty hand movement. In both instances, these attempts provide the opening for the defender's irimi. Study the defender's block of the attacker's second yokomen and the *do* that follows. Their execution should teach you much about the proper movement in sankyo and about how nage should relate uke's arm to nage's center. (Uke: Fernando Salazar)

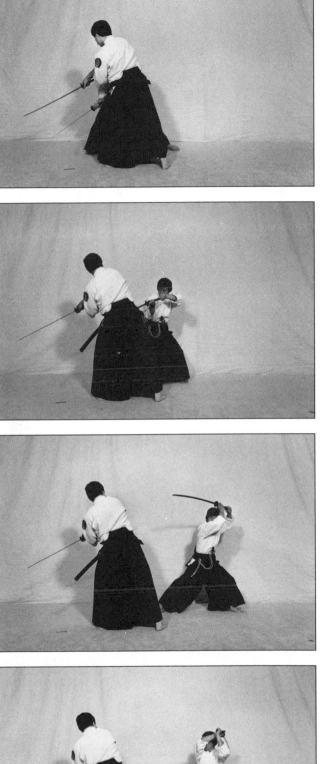

Yokomenuchi yonkyo. See the captions for shomenuchi yonkyo omote and ura (pp. 75–76) for a detailed explanation of yonkyo. Aside from the initial block and cut used here, which is typical of ikkyo-based techniques from a yokomen attack, the execution of yokomenuchi yonkyo is the same as that of shomenuchi yonkyo. (Uke: Don Moock)

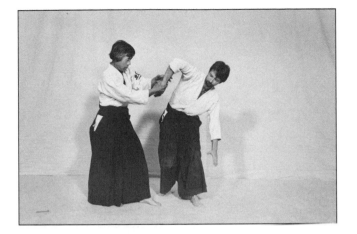

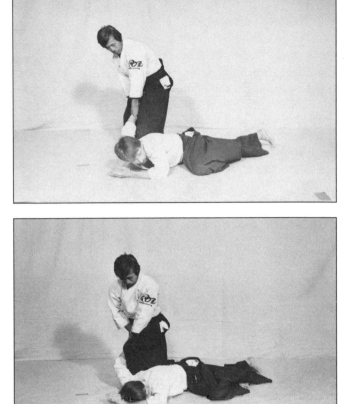

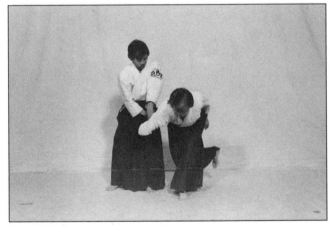

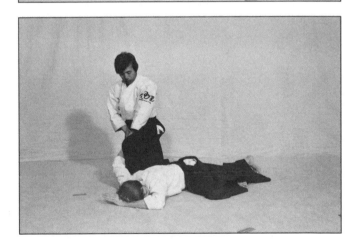

Yokomenuchi iriminage omote. In this version of yokome-nuchi iriminage, nage's movement continues in the same direction throughout the technique. The throw at the end is similar to a koshinage; nage throws uke over his hip, causing uke to take a high breakfall. It is important in throws of this kind that both nage and uke be careful to protect uke's neck. There is a real danger of injury if the throw is done—or the fall taken—improperly. (Uke: Don Moock)

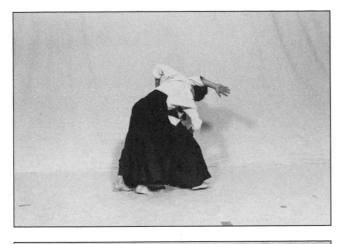

Yokomenuchi iriminage ura. Here nage reverses the direction of his movement after the initial block. The initial block is interesting in this technique. Note how nage's hand pushes under uke's, turning uke's body and creating the opening for nage to step behind uke. Nage finishes with the same koshinagelike throw used in the previous technique. The same warning about caring for uke's neck applies here. Nage's movement must be harmonious and smooth, not aggressive. Control and care for one's partner are necessary in Aikido practice. Many of these techniques in their original form were designed to break bones and cause severe injuries. (Uke: Don Moock)

Kumitachi yokomen tsuki irimi. After blocking the attacker's initial yokomen, the defender drops his sword, giving an opening for the attacker to deliver a munetsuki, or thrust to the chest. The defender then uses the energy of the forward thrust to irimi to the attacker's rear. The movement in this technique with swords is comparable to empty hand yokomenuchi iriminage. (Uke: Fernando Salazar)

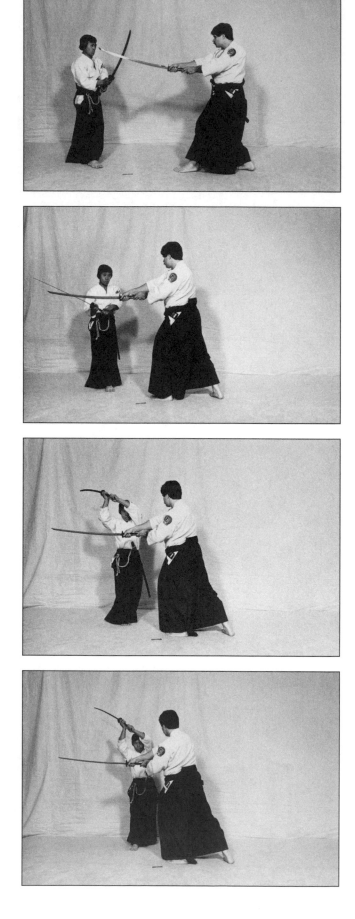

Kumitachi yokomen tsuki irimi. This kumitachi relates to empty hand yokomenuchi iriminage. After the defender has blocked the attacker's initial yokomen, the attacker attempts a tsuki to the defender's side. The defender absorbs the power of the tsuki with his block and moves behind the attacker to cut. Note the circularity of both the defender's block and his movement behind the attacker. (Uke: Fernando Salazar)

Yokomenuchi shihonage omote. Notice how nage's initial response mirrors uke's yokomenuchi. Nage uses both his hands in this technique as he blocks; one defends against uke's strike and the other covers uke's center. Nage's cut down draws uke off balance and into position for the throw. The final body and arm movement that nage uses to execute the shihonage is similar to a shomen strike with the sword. It is important to notice that as nage enters and passes under uke's arm to make the throw in this technique, nage's arms never go behind his head but must stay in front of him. Otherwise it would be easy for uke to pull him down from behind. (Uke: Don Moock)

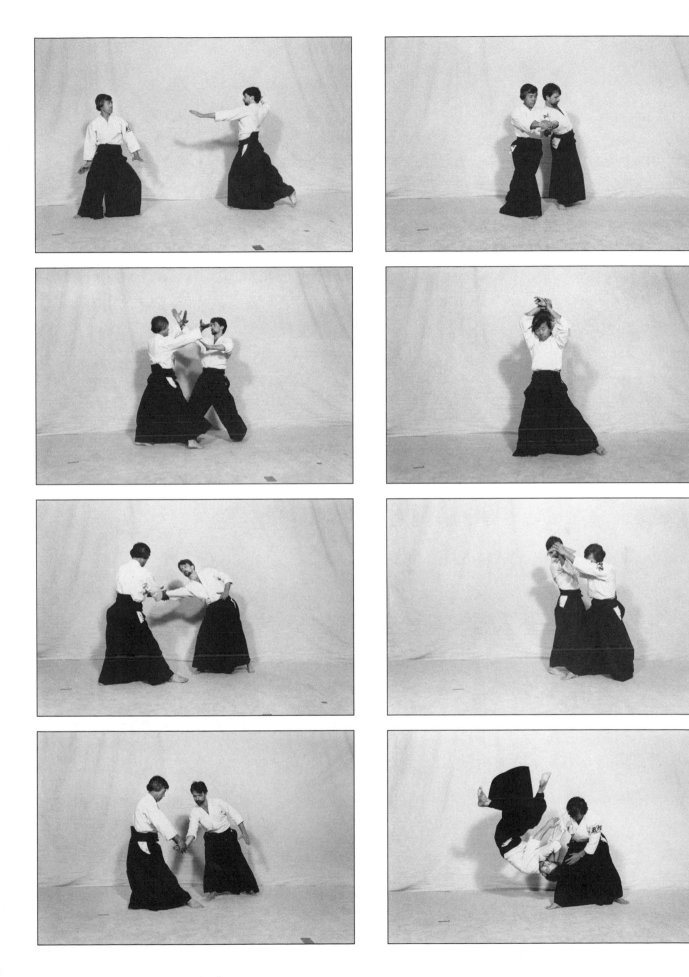

Kumitachi yokomen shomen shihonage. This kumitachi is the equivalent of empty hand yokomenuchi shihonage. The defender's irimi and *do* in response to the attacker's shomen and the defender's final cut parallel the movements used to execute the empty hand shihonage. (Uke: Fernando Salazar)

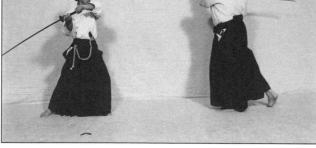

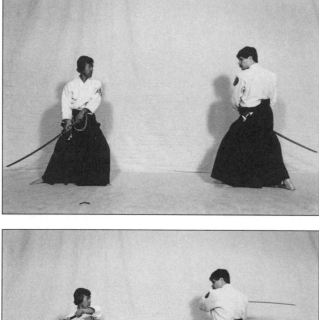

Yokomenuchi kotegaeshi (detail). In this close-up of yoko-menuchi kotegaeshi it is easy to see how nage uses both hands to execute this technique and how his hand movement is unified with his body movement. As nage blocks uke's yokomen with one hand, his other hand strikes the side of uke's head. Both hands continue in a downward curve along uke's striking arm. Notice that nage does not attempt to grab uke's hand until the very end of the technique. Also note that nage lowers his body along with his hands to bring uke off balance, rather than just pulling with his arms. (Uke: Don Moock)

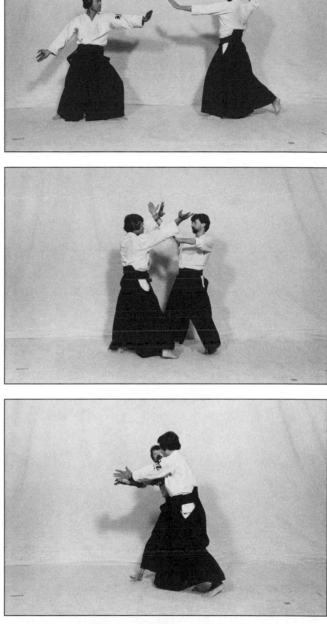

Yokomenuchi kotegaeshi. This version of yokomenuchi kotegaeshi begins with an irimi-tenkan entry. Compare this with the following version, which uses a more direct irimi entry. (Uke: Don Moock)

Yokomenuchi kotegaeshi. In this version of yokomenuchi kotegaeshi, nage goes directly for uke's center, rather than first blocking uke's strike. As nage changes hanmi, he cuts uke's striking arm downward. Note that nage guards himself against the possibility of a second strike throughout the technique, first with his outside hand as he is bringing uke into position for the throw and then with the kotegaeshi itself. Nage does not turn his back to uke, nor does he become obsessed with achieving the wrist lock but instead covers uke's whole body. If you look at the relative position of nage and uke in the second-to-last photograph, you will see how nage uses the kotegaeshi as a potential block by keeping it between himself and uke. (Uke: Don Moock)

118

Kumitachi yokomen kotegaeshi. This kumitachi relates to empty hand yokomenuchi kotegaeshi omote. The use of swords emphasizes the importance of distance and timing. Note especially that after the defender blocks the attacker's yokomen, he is careful to push the attacker's blade outside his legs before he attempts to make his cut. It is the same principle as nage's making sure to break uke's balance and turn uke's body before attempting to throw, in the empty hand version. (Uke: Fernando Salazar)

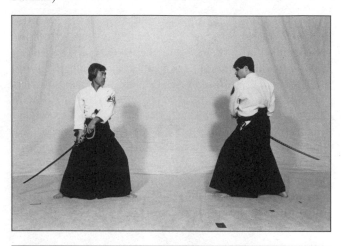

Yokomenuchi kaitenage. Kaitenage means "spinning throw." As the name of this technique indicates, circular movement is the key to its successful execution. Note the beginning block. Nage blocks and guides uke's striking hand downward and then delivers a shuto to uke's neck. A tenkan movement creates the throw itself. (Uke: Don Moock)

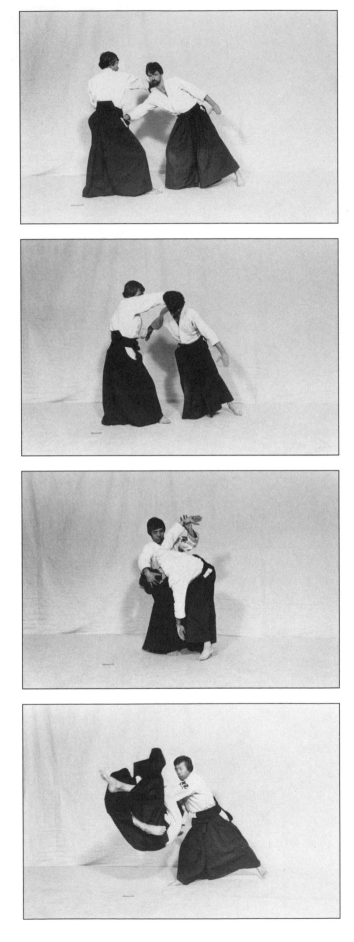

Yokomenuchi kaitenage. In this version of kaitenage, nage does not block uke's strike but ducks beneath the strike with an irimi movement. As he moves beneath uke's yokomen, he uses a hooked atemi, which strikes uke at a ninety-degree angle. Nage continues the atemi movement upward to the back of uke's neck, meanwhile blocking uke's arm with his other hand. The movement that executes the throw is again a tenkan. (Uke: Don Moock)

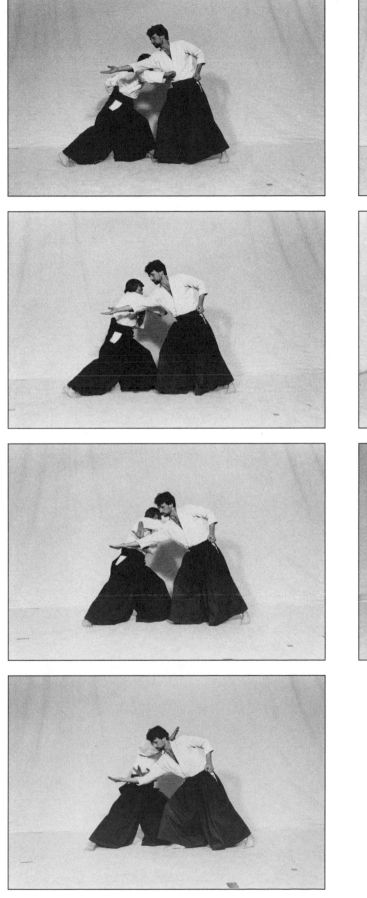

Yokomenuchi kokyunage. This technique begins with an irimi entry. (See the caption for yokomenuchi nikyo omote for an explanation of this entry.) After nage has blocked uke's strike, his hand rebounds to uke's neck for the throw. An alternate to the throw is an atemi to uke's head. In order to execute this throw, nage must turn uke's head in such a way as to make his body follow. Just yanking at uke's head will not suffice. This is another technique in which both nage and uke must be careful to protect uke's neck from injury. (Uke: Don Moock)

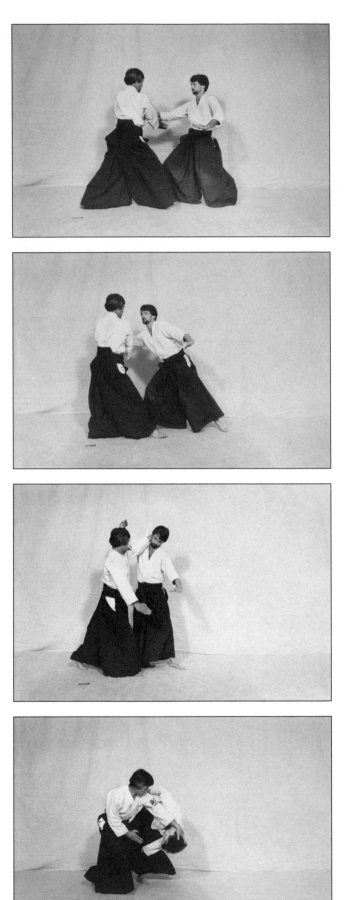

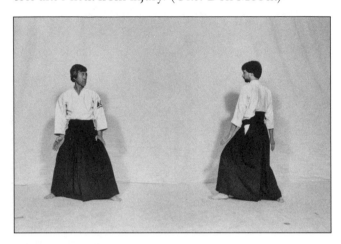

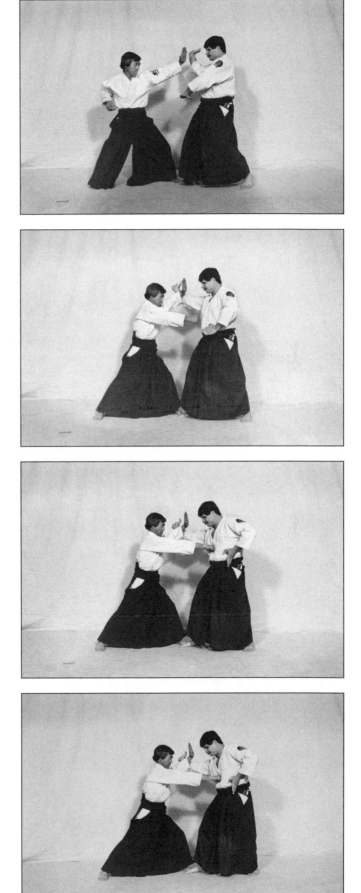

Yokomenuchi atemi points: Atemi to the solar plexus. This is a direct irimi entry where, as nage blocks uke's strike, he delivers an atemi to uke's solar plexus. In this atemiwaza, nage uses uke's momentum and direction to increase the force of his blow. As is true of the shomenuchi atemi points, you must be familiar with and be able to use atemi in order to be able to execute technique. (Uke: Fernando Salazar)

Yokomenuchi atemi points: shuto to the neck. Here you can see how defense and offense in Aikido technique often mirror each other. This series also shows the atemi potential in one of the common movements used in defense against yokomenuchi attacks. The hand with which nage is not blocking, which usually just covers uke's center, here delivers a shuto to uke's neck. (Uke: Fernando Salazar.)

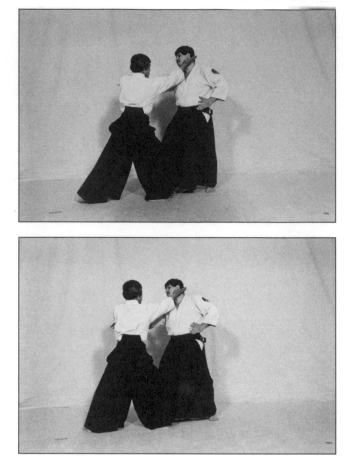

8

Techniques from Katadori

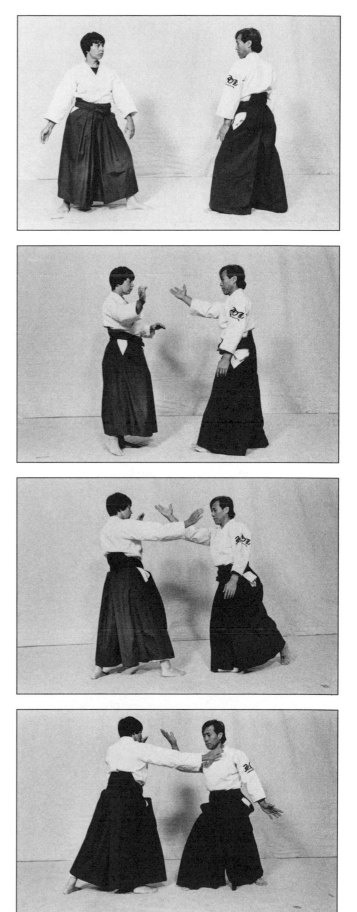

Katadori is a grab to the shoulder. As mentioned in chapter 3 it is better for beginners to start working with grabs before they work with strikes. Katadori techniques are very similar in principle to those from yokomenuchi, since the attack is coming to the upper body from the side. Yet the less threatening grab allows the beginner to work on the movement of technique with a greater feeling of safety. The practice that you do from katadori should assist you in dealing with yokomenuchi, and vice versa. And you will find that my suggestions about one will apply to the other.

Katadori ikkyo omote. In defending against katadori attacks it is important that nage deal with uke's whole body, not just the grabbing hand. It is fairly common for beginning Aikido students to become so preoccupied with breaking uke's grip that they leave themselves vulnerable in every other way. Notice here how nage defends his center with an atemi, disturbing uke's balance and then cuts down her arm to further overextend her before reaching for her hand on his shoulder. Note also how he moves off the line of her attack so that he is not open to a second attack or strike. When nage executes the ikkyo, he uses his whole body to do so. You can see how his shoulder, hip, and both arms drive into uke's center. Nage does not become fixated on uke's grip or focus just on her hand. (Uke: Wendy Whited)

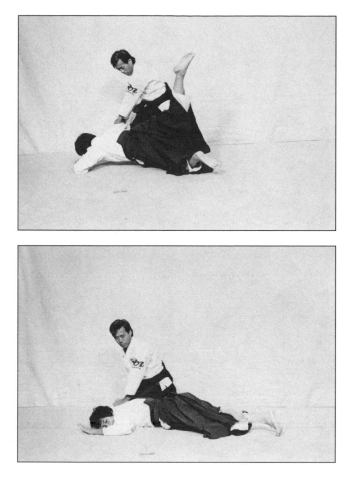

Katadori ikkyo ura. This series affords a clear view of the execution of katadori ikkyo. Note again how nage moves uke with his whole body instead of struggling with her hand. The grip that he uses on her hand once he has freed her hand from his shoulder is important for two reasons. First, nage grabs precisely. The wrist torques used in Aikido are designed to direct the body by the skillful use of mechanics rather than by inflicting pain. The exact grab here creates a wrist twist that connects with uke's whole body; a slightly different grab will not produce the same effect. (This is one of the reasons that aggression and competition in practice are detrimental to your study of Aikido. The acquisition and the understanding of knowledge are what allow you to have control of technique, not the imposition of pain on your partner. It is important to pay attention to detail and to study the structure of the human body.) The second point worth noting about nage's manipulation of uke's hand is its similarity to a *kesa giri.* Learning sword technique is an important compliment and aid to your empty hand aikido technique. It helps teach you correct movement and amplifies the direction and the feeling that causes a movement to be successful. (Uke: Wendy Whited)

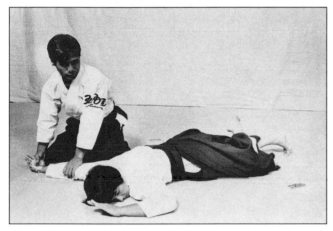

Katadori iriminage. This iriminage starts with a nikyo, which nage uses to guard against uke's next attack and to create an opening for entry. One reason that nage might choose to turn the initial nikyo into iriminage would be the presence of other attackers. Looking at the progress of this technique, you can see that the rotating movement used to make the throw allows nage to scan his surroundings and that through the greater part of the technique uke's body covers nage's front and can function as a shield. Iriminage shields the back, which is also an important function of irimi-tenkan movement. Note the way that nage keeps his attention focused on uke even after he has finished the throw, protecting himself and preventing uke from rising to attack again. (Uke: Chuck Weber)

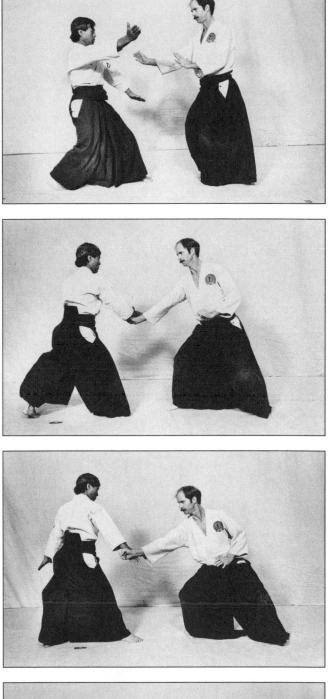

Katadori iriminage. Katadori attacks demonstrate clearly the importance of timing and distance in nage's response to attack. Here, nage moves before uke grabs. He moves so that uke cannot grab him but believes he can and so keeps trying. This is an example of musubi: nage maintains communication with his uke. As uke reaches for the grab, nage cuts uke's grabbing hand down, thus taking uke's balance and overextending him. Nage must be careful in this defense not to turn his back to uke as he is cutting down the grabbing hand. Turning his back would leave him open to a second attack. Nage must keep his focus on uke's center, not on the single limb that has made the initial attack. (Uke: Chuck Weber)

Katadori iriminage, alternative block. Usually nage blocks a katadori with the opposite rather than the mirroring hand; that is to say, one normally blocks a right-handed grab with the right hand and a left-handed one with the left. In this instance, however, nage blocks uke's katadori with the mirroring hand. Nage then cuts up under uke's arm with the other hand and turns uke's body. This gives nage the opening to enter for the iriminage. This emphasizes that you must be flexible in practicing Aikido technique. You cannot become fixated on one response to any attack but must be aware of the range of possibilities that are available. Then you must practice them till you are able, when the attack comes, to make a spontaneous decision. This block, for instance, might be used in a situation where nage has no room for the large step back usually taken to create distance between uke and nage in katadori techniques or in any situation where nage must deflect uke's attack without much movement. (Uke: Chuck Weber)

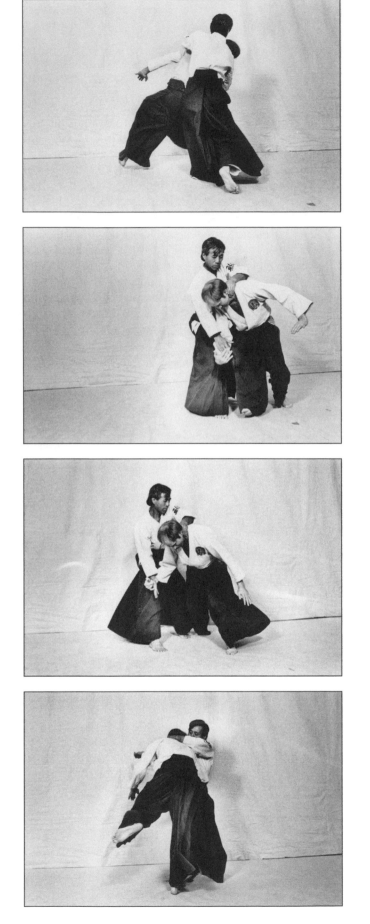

Katadori kokyunage. The timing nage uses in this technique allows uke to grab his shoulder. The initial block differs from many of the other katadori techniques shown in that nage blocks on the outside of uke's arm rather than on the inside. Nage contracts his body and arms initially to bring uke off balance and into his center and then expands to make the throw. The way that nage gathers uke's arm initially is similar to nikyo (see, e.g., chapter 9). The positioning of nage's arm must be very exact in order to break uke's balance. (Uke: Chuck Weber)

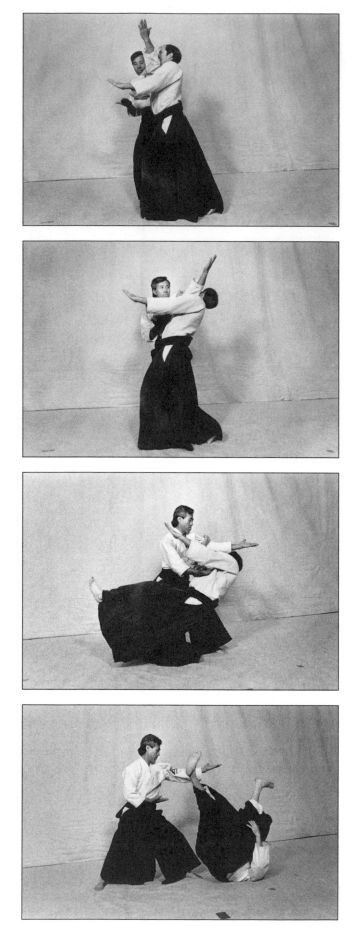

9
Techniques from Munetsuki

Munetsuki is a strike or thrust to the middle body. In empty hand techniques, this strike takes the form of a punch; in sword or jo techniques it is a thrust with the point of the weapon.

Defending against munetsuki serves the purpose of do-no-tanden, or middle-body training. The untrained person will often respond to attacks to the middle body by trying to trap the punch with his hands and pull his center out of reach of the punch. This produces a distorted posture in which the person's arms are overextended and his rear protrudes. Munetsuki training helps one to overcome this response and replace it with responses characterized by good posture and confidence.

Munetsuki ikkyo. This technique provides another example of the use of musubi. As uke punches, nage causes him to overextend and lose his balance with the initial block. Uke naturally attempts to retract his punch and regain his balance, and nage uses his reaction to move in for ikkyo. In each case nage is using uke's movement, rather than fighting it. (Uke: Kevin Choate)

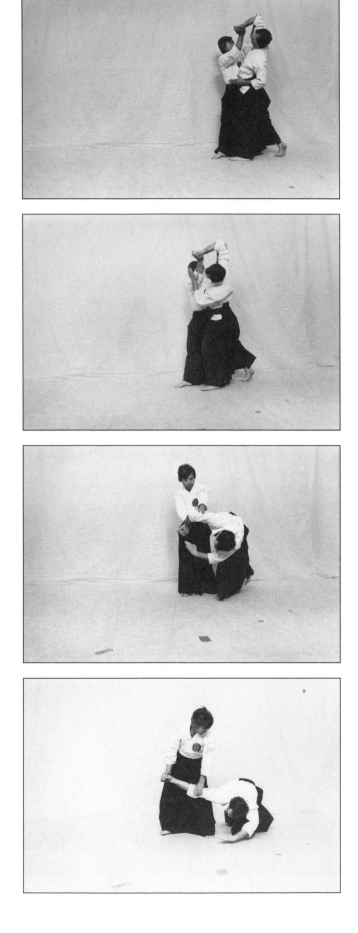

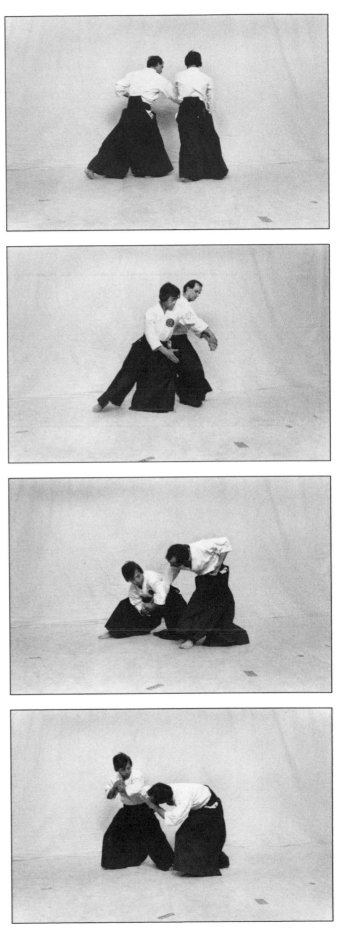

Munetsuki nikyo. Since the success of Aikido technique depends on communication between the participants—in that nage responds to and uses uke's movement rather than fighting against it—it stands to reason that the movements in technique must be continuous. To stop a movement means to stop uke's energy and allow him or her to regain balance and position. Continuous movement implies circular movement, whereas linear movement tends to separate itself into a collection of stops and starts. In the technique depicted here, munetsuki nikyo, one can see clearly the chain of circles and spirals that make nage's control of uke possible. The initial circle is centrifugal, as nage uses the irimi-tenkan movement to extend the force of uke's punch out and then in a circle around his periphery. Concurrently, nage changes his movement to a centripetal, upward spiral, which twists uke's punching arm into the nikyo hold at nage's center. The accomplishment of the final pin repeats this pattern of extension and contraction. You might image it as a whirlpool caused by a sinking ship, where the water has first flooded out displaced by the weight of the ship, and then spirals inward to fill the empty space caused by the ship's descent. (Uke: Kevin Choate)

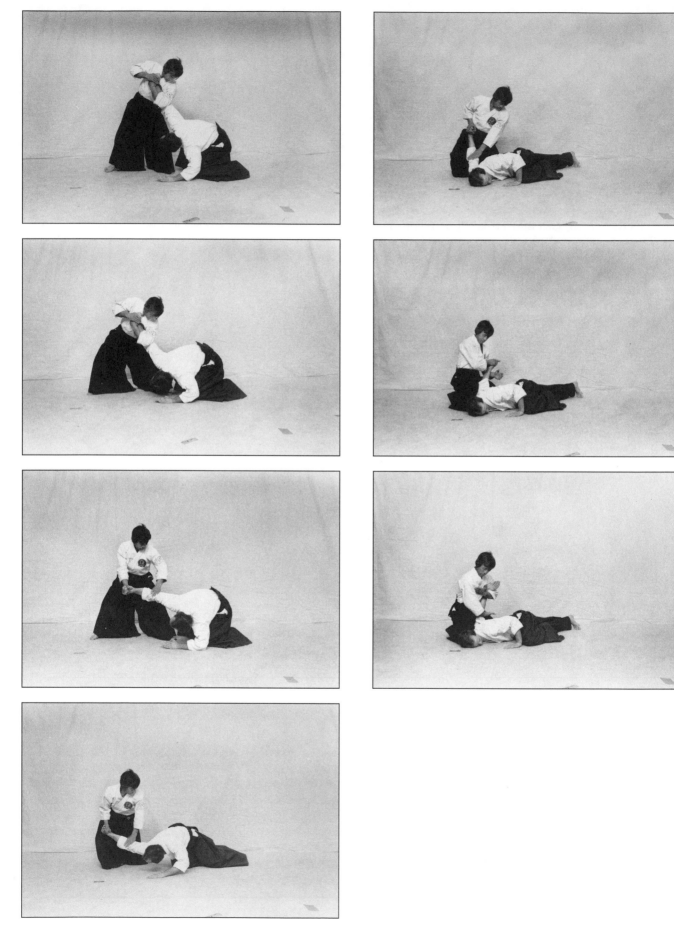

Munetsuki sankyo. This technique, like the previously shown tsuki nikyo, consists of a series of spirals. In this case, after the initial irimi-tenkan movement, nage's first spiral is inward and upward, followed by the outward and downward spiral that brings uke to the floor. Although sankyo uses the wrist and elbow to control uke, the success of this technique is not dependent on inflicting pain to uke's wrist but on how well nage can connect with and control uke's center. In any Aikido technique, no matter what part of uke's body is the vehicle for control, nage's goal is to control uke's center. (Uke: Kevin Choate)

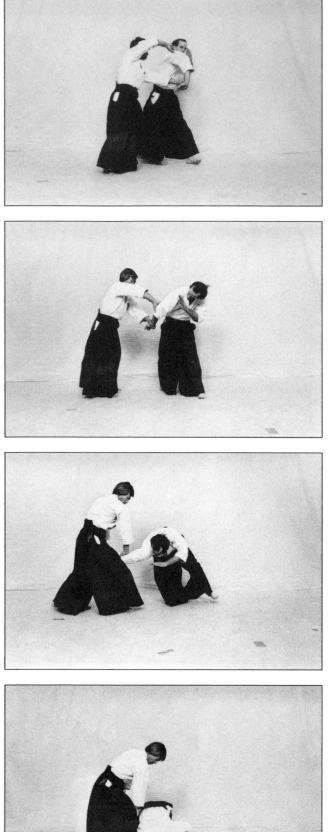

Munetsuki iriminage. In this version of iriminage, nage uses no tenkan movement. After his initial irimi he moves straight in and throws. Note how tightly nage covers uke's center before he deflects the trajectory of uke's punch. (Uke: Chuck Weber)

Munetsuki kotegaeshi. As uke attempts to punch, nage immediately covers and defends the center, rather than focusing on the striking hand. Uke's reaction to this alters the timing of the movement just enough to allow nage to take command of the movement, capturing uke's wrist and performing a tenkan movement that takes nage safely to uke's rear. It is important in performing this movement not to kill the power of uke's attack but to use it, instead. Note how uke follows nage, attempting to regain his full balance, with his hand at the ready for a second strike, in case the opportunity should present itself. The final throw, kotegaeshi, uses a wrist twist that is the same spiral as—but in the opposite direction from—nikyo. (Uke: Kevin Choate)

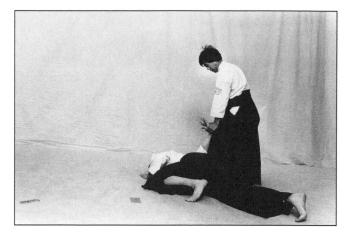

Munetsuki kaitenage. The initial movement in this technique is an irimi. As nage enters to uke's outside, nage's lower hand guides uke's punch downward while allowing it to continue in its original direction. Nage's upper hand crosses behind uke's neck. Nage then makes a tenkan, bringing uke's head down and his arm up. Movement in this "spinning throw" must be circular. Nage's tenkan creates a horizontal circle, while he simultaneously rotates uke in a vertical circle. Nage's footwork is nothing more than irimi-tenkan. (Uke: Kevin Choate)

Kumitachi tsuki irimi. This kumitachi corresponds to the previously shown empty hand munetsuki kaitenage. Here, after the defender makes an irimi and blocks the attacker's tsuki, he brings his sword around his head in a circular movement for the final kesa giri to the back of the neck. The rotating movement that the defender uses to move from the block to the final cut corresponds to the full tenkan from block to throw in the empty hand movement. In the kumitachi version, the defender's hands *must* move in unison because both hands hold the sword. In the empty hand version of kaitenage you should keep the same feeling of unity between the hands, even though they are physically separated. (Uke: Patricia Saotome)

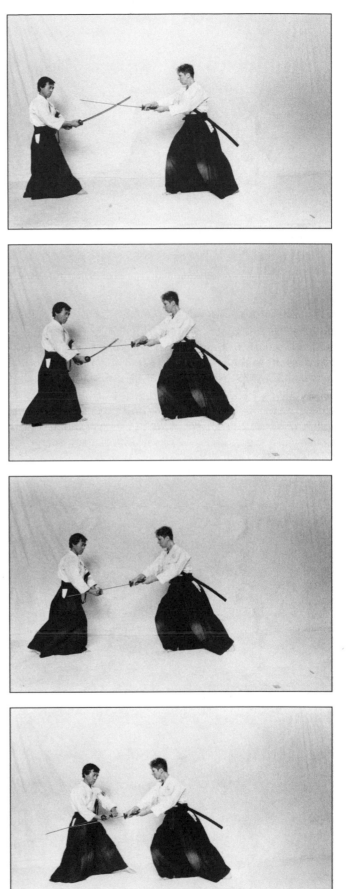

Munetsuki kaitenage (variation). This variation on munetsuki kaitenage shows an alternative available to nage should uke try to escape at the point of the throw. As uke attempts to spin out of the throw, nage follows his movement, using uke's arm as a lever and putting pressure on uke's neck. This allows nage to retain control of uke. The execution of this throw emphasizes that good communication between nage and uke must be maintained throughout the technique and that nage's choice of throw at the end must not be arbitrary but must be made in response to uke's movement. (Uke: Kevin Choate)

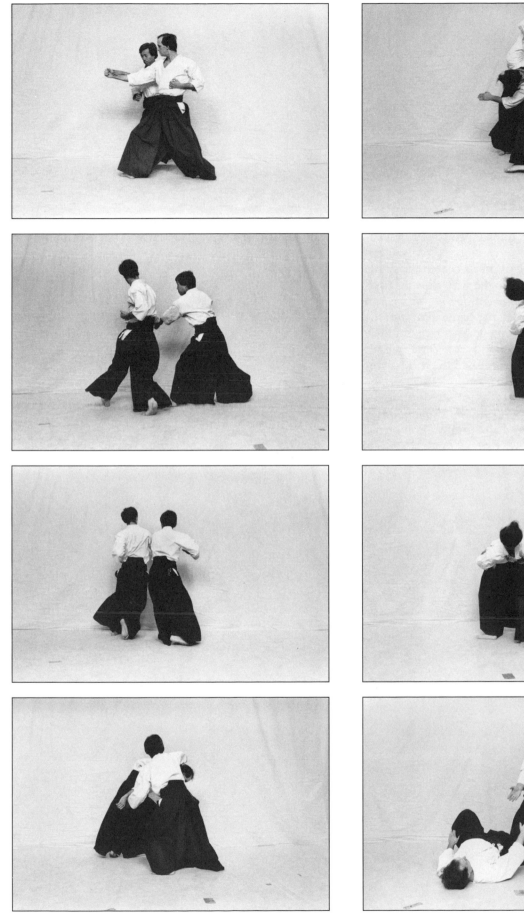

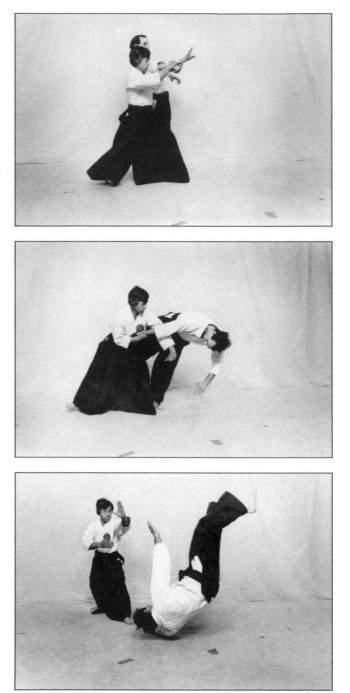

Munetsuki kokyunage. This technique provides a clear example of irimi-tenkan principle at work. First, you can see how nage enters, controlling uke's center and drawing uke's punch, and then spins to the side, allowing uke's strike to pass him. The whole technique is one smooth movement. Note how nage, at the same time that he makes his tenkan, positions himself to throw. You may also observe that nage never allows his concentration and focus to waver even after he has finished the throw. This is an illustration of zanshin, or the continuous awareness of one's surroundings. Also worthy of attention is the ukemi in this technique. The fourth photograph in this series shows a good example of the proper position for beginning a forward roll. (Uke: Kevin Choate)

Munetsuki koshinage. This is an advanced technique, but it provides an important illustration—for Aikido students of any level—of the significance of timing, movement, and communication in Aikido technique. To accomplish this throw, nage does *not* lift up his uke and throw him. This would be difficult if not impossible. Rather, nage uses continuous movement to cause his uke to fall over him. This koshinage begins with nage using irimi-tenkan movement to diffuse the energy of uke's attack in a centrifugal circle, with nage at the axis and uke on the periphery. At the proper moment, nage turns into uke's center with an atemi to uke's face. The atemi opens up uke's body and destroys his balance, creating the space for nage to move in and throw. Note that from the atemi on, uke remains extended and overbalanced and that nage is collected and low. As nage moves through uke beneath uke's center of gravity, uke is forced to fall over nage. The principle is similar to that of a wave breaking over a rock. The key to accomplishing this technique is continuous and well-coordinated movement. (Uke: Kevin Choate)

10

Techniques from Katatedori

Katatedori is a grab to the wrist. Katatedori are perhaps the most commonly used attacks in beginning training in Aikido. One reason for this, as I have said, is to give beginners the opportunity to physically feel the principles behind Aikido technique and to allow them to alter the aggressive and fearful manner in which they are accustomed to respond to threat. Katatedori techniques present a fruitful opportunity for the beginner to study timing, distance, position, and the details of the mechanics of the body.

However, katatedori, like shomenuchi, while not very dangerous in their present form, have their origin in very severe training. Katatedori are based on situations in which samurai grabbed the hand of an armed opponent to prevent him from drawing his sword. Again, let me say that it is important to respond to your partner in Aikido practice as if he were armed and capable of doing you fatal harm. When you study katatedori techniques, do not think of the attacks as "unrealistic." Instead, concentrate on learning to perceive both your own and your partners' weak points and then use this knowledge to enhance your practice and your understanding.

Katatedori ikkyo omote. This ikkyo omote shows clearly the centripetal power that omote techniques employ. You can see that the power of uke's attack is diffused in a spiral that decreases in size. Uke is collected into nage's center. Also worth noting is how nage reflects the movement of uke in order to execute the technique. After nage has drawn uke off balance, she naturally desires to rise and regain her balance. Nage uses uke's movement to move against her center. He uses her instinct for recovery, rather than fighting against it. (Uke: Wendy Whited)

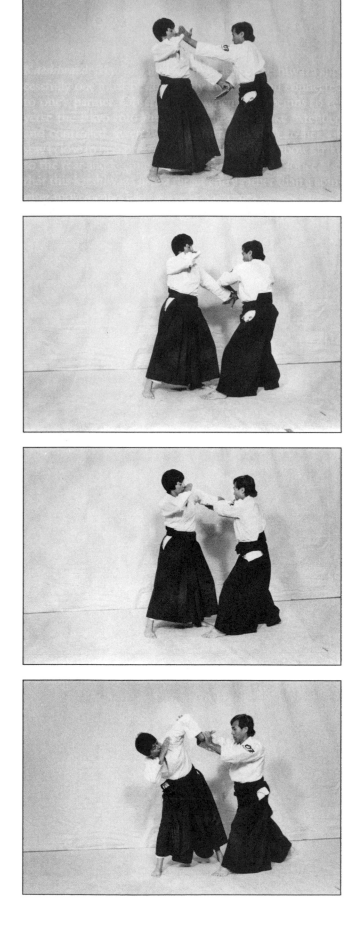

Katatedori ikkyo ura. It is easy to see in this series of photographs how nage moves off the line of uke's attack and uses atemi to make himself safe from a second attack. The ura movement used in this ikkyo serves two purposes. First, it allows nage to protect his back by using a circular throw. Second, uke resisting an omote movement, nage changes direction rather than fighting against the resistance. The way uke is spun around in a circle with nage as the axis is typical of ura movement. (Uke: Wendy Whited)

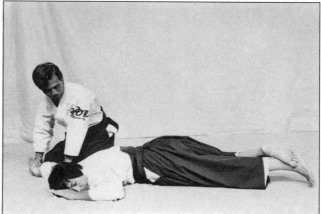

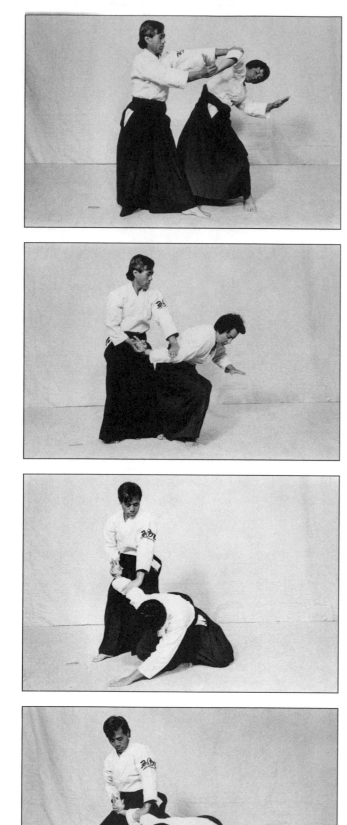

Katatedori iriminage. It is important to remember that nage, when grabbed, should not be passive. Originally a grab in practice was often prompted by a strike and was used as a defense (as in the jo ikkyo from empty hand grab in chapter 5). You can see here how nage's extended hand guards his center from the beginning of the technique. As he receives the force of uke's attack, he maintains the pressure on her center; he does not allow his arm to collapse. Observe how she is directed off the line of her attack. Nage's hand also guards him and covers his head as he moves behind uke. In this version of iriminage, there is no spinning or tenkan movement. Nage merely moves in, breaks uke's balance, and throws. (Uke: Wendy Whited)

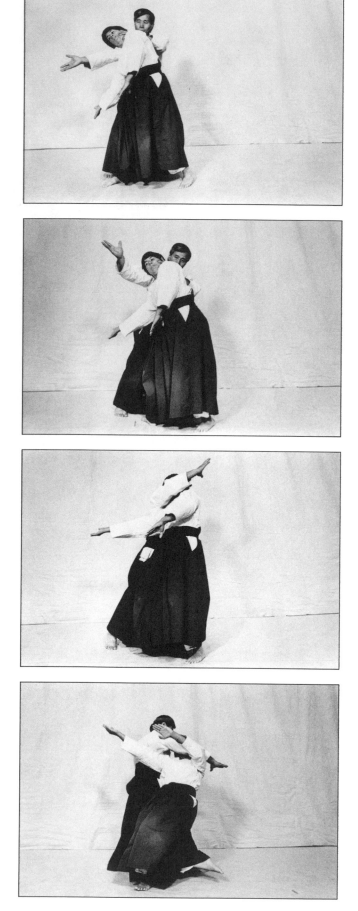

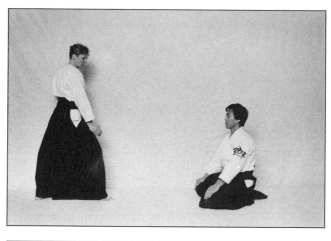

Hanmi handachi katatedori shihonage. Hanmi handachi techniques, like suwariwaza techniques, derived from the samurais' need to protect themselves if attacked when sitting in seiza. Note how, as uke grabs, nage's hands rise in a kokyu tanden ho movement to protect his head from a strike and his leg nearest uke comes up to protect his body from a kick. (Uke: Patricia Saotome)

Kumiiai hanmi handachi shomen shihonage. This kumiiai is the equivalent of empty hand hanmi handachi shihonage. The use of swords makes it easy to see the origin of hanmi handachi techniques from when sword fighting was a way of life. Here the defender moves directly in under the attacker's shomen because there is no other safe place to go. A standing antagonist can easily track a seated one who attempts to escape. The defender's initial entry well illustrates the principle of ikkyo and irimi, that to meet an attack fearlessly and take over the attacker's center affords nage the greatest chance of survival. (Uke: Fernando Salazar)

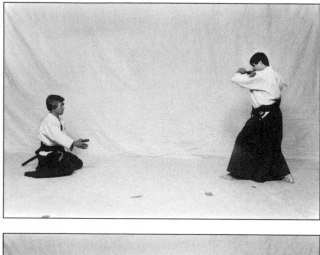

11

Techniques from Ryotemochi

Ryotemochi is a two-handed grab. In all of the techniques shown uke grabs both of nage's hands with both of hers. (Ryotemochi can also indicate that uke grabs one of nage's hands with both hands.) In practicing the variety of ryotemochi techniques used here, it is important to remember that the reason people grab in such a fashion is to immobilize their opponent in order to deliver a second, more aggressive attack, probably a kick. In all of the ensuing ryotemochi techniques, therefore, getting off the line of attack is emphasized. Even if a second attack like a kick is not being used in practice, you must train yourself to always move so that you would protect yourself if it were. It is important to expand your martial awareness.

tus of the attack. The upward hand has the effect of directing uke's energy centrifugally, and the downward hand directs it centripetally. The combined movement of the two hands creates a void into which uke falls. This throw cannot be accomplished without nage's completely harmonizing with uke's movement. Tenchinage is also composed of a series of circles: the large, horizontal circle that nage creates with his body movement and the two smaller, simultaneously constructed spirals that nage creates with his hands, one ascending and one descending. Note the shape of nage's hands as he makes these spirals and mark the similarity of their shape to that in kokyu tanden ho (chapter 3). (Uke: Patricia Saotome)

Ryotemochi tenchinage. The name *tenchinage* means "Heaven-and-Earth throw." It is so named because nage diffuses the energy of uke's attack by spiraling one hand upward toward Heaven and one hand downward, toward Earth. Tenchinage illustrates many essential points about how Aikido technique works. Nage must receive uke's unified energy with both hands. As nage retreats, absorbing the force of uke's attack, you can observe how both of his hands twist outward, diffusing around him the impe-

Ryotemochi tenchinage. This series of photographs shows a different application of ryotemochi tenchinage. Here nage grabs uke's head, bending it downward and turning it underneath for the final throw. Uke remains alert to the possible variations on techniques and to how her own openings influence nage's choice as to which variation of a throw to use. (Uke: Patricia Saotome)

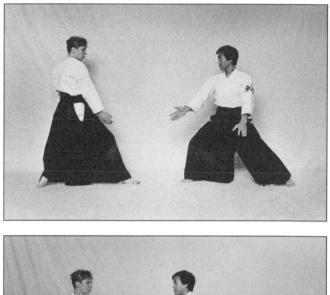

Ryotemochi shihonage. Here nage uses a tenkan movement to take himself off the line of uke's attack. Many people, when executing this movement, will attempt to drag uke off balance, when in fact that is an extremely ineffective approach. Instead, nage rotates uke around the axis of her own center. This makes it easy for him to deflect uke's attack and take her balance. (Uke: Patricia Saotome)

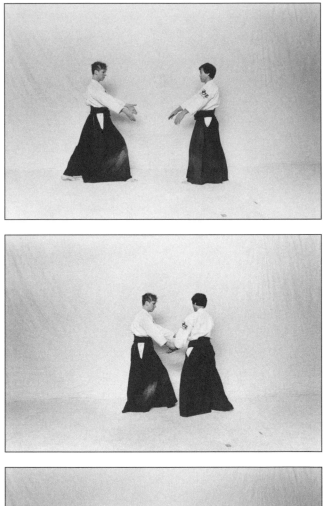

Ryotemochi kokyunage. This technique provides an excellent illustration of how the principles of kokyu tanden ho work in motion (see chapter 3). Nage's initial hand movements are the same in both techniques. Kokyunage, like kokyu tanden ho, works through musubi. Nage does not use logic to execute this technique; he does not have time. He instead *responds* to the movement of uke. He goes with the direction of her attack. Here uke is pushing forward. Nage absorbs her forward motion, at the same time lifting her center of balance and opening her up. Her energy is diffused around nage. Nage then enters the opening he has created, dropping to the ground as he moves to uke's rear. Uke continues forward, and the dropping of nage's weight brings her down into the fall as she passes above him. Nage's success depends on his ability to remain relaxed, stable, and confident. If he were stiff, he would not be able to feel and respond to uke's movement; and if he were nervous or doubtful of himself he would be too hesitant about his reactions to move decisively. Aggressiveness impedes kokyunage because it destroys the possibility of communication. (Uke: Patricia Saotome)

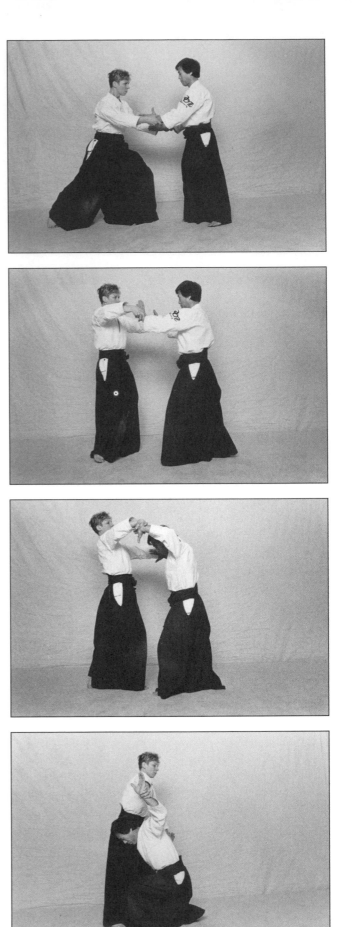

Ryotemochi kokyunage. In this version of kokyunage, nage uses an outside irimi to take himself off the line of attack. He combines this with a kokyu hand movement that takes uke's balance and also uses her arms, as well as his own, to guard against further attack. Uke's lower arm, which nage has drawn across uke's body, guards against kicks. To execute the throw, nage brings uke's upper arm down and across her lower body. Thus uke, until she is thrown, is effectively tied up in her own arms. It is important to note that although this movement appears superficially different from the previous kokyunage, it is the same movement in all its essential points. It uses the same kokyu movement of the hands, this time on the outside of uke's wrists. It uses the principle of musubi in responding to uke's attack, and it uses the same extension and dropping of nage's weight to execute the throw. (Uke: Patricia Saotome)

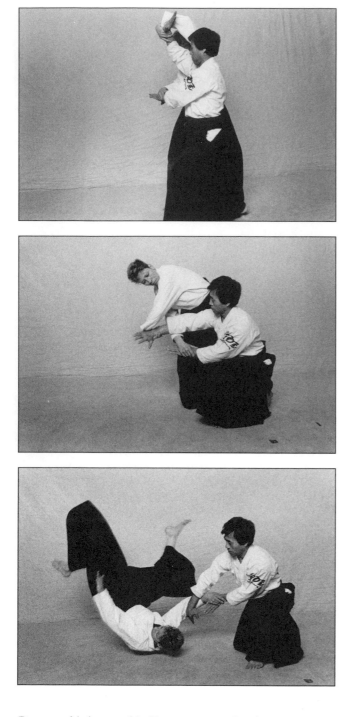

Ryotemochi kotegaeshi. You must maintain a constant awareness of your position in relation to your partner and of the significance of that position. Here, as soon as uke starts to grab, nage makes an irimi, which takes him off the line of attack. He continues to maintain a safe position throughout the rest of the technique. In the eighth and ninth photographs in this series, you can see very clearly the way that nage grabs uke's hand for the kotegaeshi. Two points are worth observing about this grab. First, it is not like the normal grab used to create kotegaeshi but rather like the one you would use on your own wrist in kotegaeshi wrist exercises. Second, compare this kotegaeshi with nikyo and notice that they use the same spiral but in opposite directions. (Uke: Patricia Saotome)

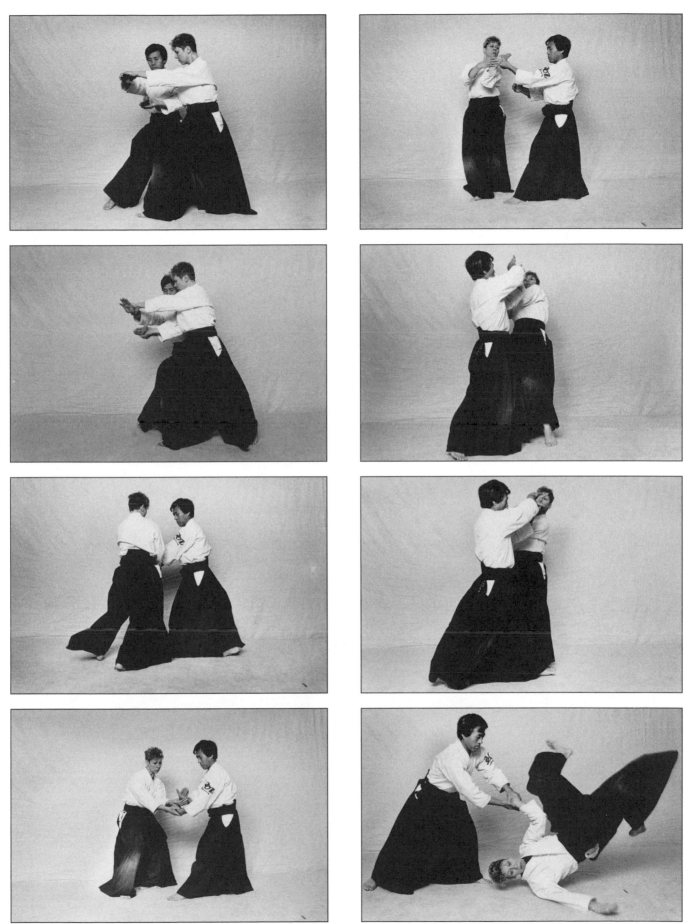

12

Techniques from Kosadori and Ushirowaza

Ushirowaza, or techniques from the rear, offer an opportunity to study the defense of your back. Originally ushirowaza were not practiced separately from techniques done from frontal attacks but were employed by nage if uke succeeded in getting behind him. Although we generally practice ushirowaza as a separate category of techniques today, it is important to remember their relationship to techniques done from other attacks. This relationship is easy to see when you look at techniques from kosadori, or cross-hand grabs, since the conventional variety of ushirowaza techniques begin with a kosadori. This chapter begins with techniques from kosadori and continues with ushirowaza. Please compare the two types of techniques and observe for yourself how the former can lead into the latter.

Ushirowaza (Uke: Bruce Merkle; photograph by P. Saotome)

Kosadori iriminage. This provides a good example of the importance of nage's remaining in a neutral frame of mind, receptive to uke's attack. As uke grabs, nage must be able to feel the direction and force of uke's attack and react accordingly. Anticipating or struggling against uke's attack will interfere with nage's perception. Here nage uses the spinal movement of his arm to direct uke off the line of attack and to break his balance. Nage's arm must be relaxed but strong; it cannot be either stiff or collapsed. This throw works through the unification, not the opposition, of uke's and nage's energies. (Uke: Chuck Weber)

Kosadori iriminage. In the course of your Aikido practice, you will encounter many different types of behaviors and body structures in your partners. One approach to a technique will not work in all situations or against all people. In this version of kosadori iriminage, nage uses a big body movement, first to get behind uke and then to take uke's balance. This approach might be used in a situation where uke was stiff or resistant and did not allow nage to push or pull. Nage employs his whole body weight to break uke's balance. Note how low nage sinks as he brings uke down. (Uke: Chuck Weber)

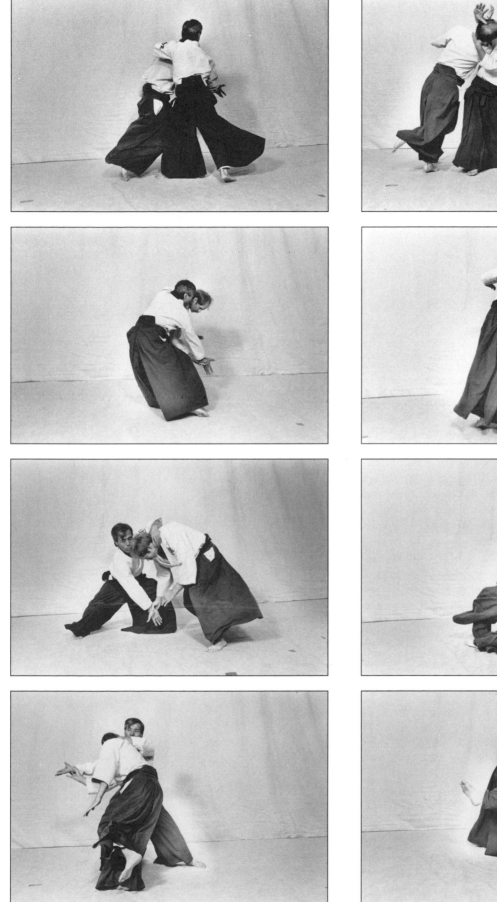

174

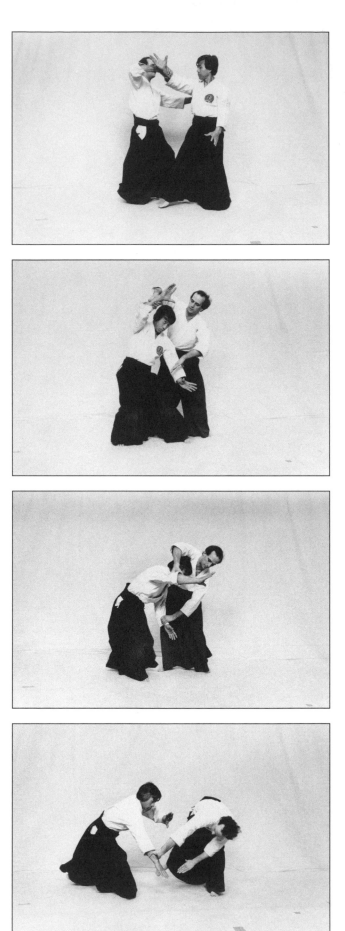

Ushirowaza nikyo. Ushirowaza demonstrate the importance of the role of the uke and of good ukemi in Aikido training since the attack here requires so much activity on the part of the uke. First, uke must understand the intent of the attack. Uke grabs nage's outstretched arm to defend against potential attack. Uke attempts to grab nage from behind because nage's front is covered, with no openings for attack. Uke's effort to get around nage's back and grab the other arm must be direct and purposeful, the goal being to immobilize nage. One often sees a beginning Aikido student, as uke in ushirowaza, hang on to nage's arm and run around in an aimless circle. This not only makes the technique difficult for nage to execute but makes it meaningless, for there is then really no attack to respond to. Uke must be aware of the purpose of the attack and of the situation uke is trying to create for nage, so that nage may have useful practice. (Uke: Kevin Choate)

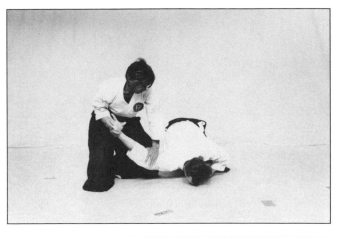

Ushirowaza shihonage. In the technique pictured here, ushirowaza shihonage, we see clear examples—in both nage's response to uke's attack and in his execution of the shihonage throw—of how irimi-tenkan blends together into one smooth movement, rather than being separate steps. (Uke: Kevin Choate)

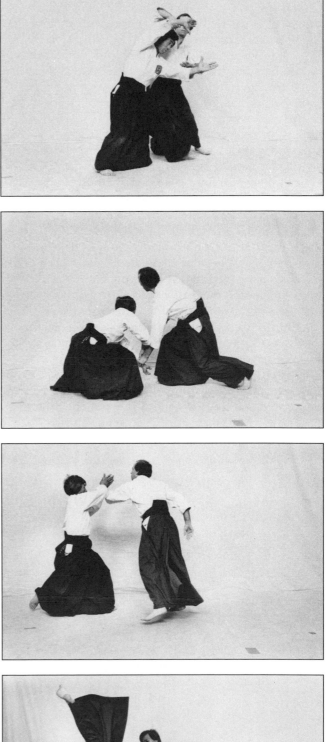

Ushirowaza kotegaeshi. In this technique the timing of nage's movement differs from some of those previously shown. Here nage does not allow uke to grab him fully from behind but uses an irimi movement to go through the opening that uke has created by his attempt to get behind nage. Note the tenkan movement and the full use of the body that nage employs to execute the final throw. (Uke: Kevin Choate)

Ushirowaza kokyunage. In the form of ushirowaza we see here, uke is forced by nage's threatened atemi to block nage's hand and try to go behind nage's back. Remember that ushirowaza relates closely to kosadori and that both should be motivated by uke's need to block a threatened atemi by nage. The timing of uke's attack and nage's response determines both which avenue of attack uke will pursue and what nage's response will be. In this technique—ushirowaza kokyunage—uke succeeds in grabbing and lowering nage's threatening hand and in getting completely behind uke and grabbing him. Again we see, even in this apparently invidious situation for nage, that nage uses both the direction and the intent of uke's attack to execute the technique, rather than fighting it. As uke grabs nage and attempts to compress him, nage contracts and continues to turn in the direction in which uke has been moving. This causes uke to become stretched around nage's concentrated center, like a tire around a wheel. As the centrifugal power of nage's turn gains force, nage opens up in the direction of his turn with one arm, keeping uke tied to his center with the other arm. This results finally in uke flying outward and falling, while nage remains balanced in the center. It is worthwhile also to note the similarity of the hand movement in this technique to that in tenchinage. The lower hand creates a downward and inward spiral, while the upper hand spirals outward and skyward. (Uke: Kevin Choate)

Ushirowaza koshinage. As in the previously described ushirowaza, uke defends against nage's threat of atemi and attempts to grab nage from behind, and nage becomes the axis around which uke is forced to revolve. Remember from the earlier description of munetsuki koshinage that nage must move through uke's center of balance rather than attempting to lift uke, in order to execute a koshinage (chapter 9). Note that nage keeps uke overextended throughout the duration of this technique. (Uke: Kevin Choate)

13

Advanced
Techniques

As the Aikido student advances, he or she will begin to apply the knowledge and the skills acquired to more and more challenging situations and problems. I have mentioned jiu-waza, in which nage responds with spontaneous movement to attacks that may or may not be prearranged. There is also randori, in which nage defends against multiple attackers. Another form of advanced training are kaeshiwaza, or reversal techniques. In kaeshiwaza, several techniques are practiced in a series of reversals. Each technique leads into the next, and uke and nage may exchange roles a number of times before the kaeshiwaza is ended. In this chapter there is a small sampling of empty hand kaeshiwaza and two sword kata employing a similar concept. To practice kaeshiwaza you must develop a heightened sense of awareness to your partners and the physical and mental relationship between you and them. I hope that these techniques will give the reader some idea of the practice principles that Aikido strives to realize.

Tantodori

Kaeshiwaza: ikkyo into nikyo irimi. This is a relatively simple example of kaeshiwaza, involving only two techniques. Uke attempts ikkyo. Nage receives her energy and uses the direction and impetus of her movement to draw her off balance and reestablish his control. He then proceeds into a nikyo irimi. Kaeshiwaza provides an excellent example of how ukemi works not only for self-protection but also for maintaining connection to one's partner and keeping opportunities open for further techniques. Kaeshiwaza is also excellent training in musubi, timing, balance, and awareness. Notice here how nage remains in the center of the movement, while uke is forced to circle around him. (Uke: Patricia Saotome)

.

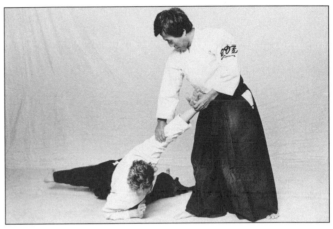

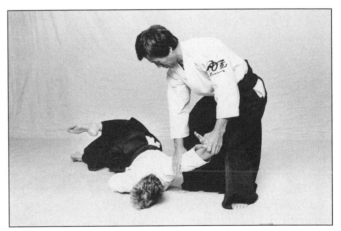

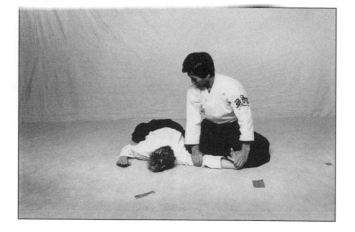

Kaeshiwaza: ikkyo into nikyo ura. Kaeshiwaza blurs the line between uke and nage, attack and defense, emphasizing the point that attack and defense are not separate but the same. Observe how this series appears to begin with a simultaneous coming together of uke and nage rather than a specific defense and attack. (Uke: Patricia Saotome)

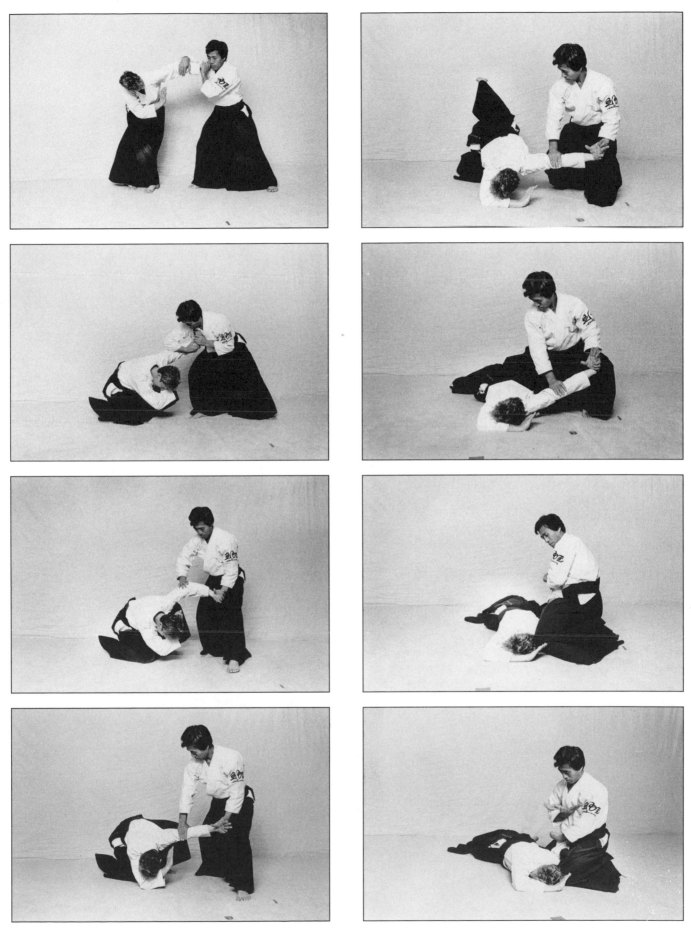

Kaeshiwaza: ikkyo into sankyo. To practice kaeshiwaza successfully one must be constantly aware of and connected to one's partner. Observe how, when nage begins to reverse the ikkyo into the sankyo, he keeps uke extended and controlled. Even when he turns his back to her, he stays close to her, protecting himself with an elbow strike to the rear and keeping her on the defensive. Notice also that this kaeshiwaza uses a direct entry rather than a spinning movement. (Uke: Patricia Saotome)

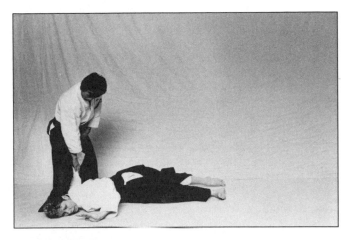

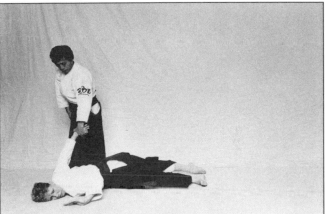

Kumitachi shomen uke nagashi kesa giri. As the defender blocks the attacker's shomen, the attacker presses down on the block. The defender takes advantage of that pressure, allowing attacker's sword to slide off of his as he moves in to make the final kesa giri. This kumitachi relates to empty hand shomenuchi ikkyo with a reversal to kokyunage in response to uke's resistance (not illustrated). (Uke: Patricia Saotome)

Kumiiai kesu giri shomen ikkyo. This kumiiai series dramatizes several important points about Aikido technique. As the defender falls back to avoid the attacker's first cut, he draws his sword. You can see that he keeps the point focused on the attacker the whole time that he is drawing. The importance of this—mentioned in connection with empty hand techniques—is made clearer by the use of swords. When the attacker makes his second cut, a shomen, the defender rises with an irimi movement to take himself out of the line of the cut and raises his sword to block. Note that the defender's block covers his head. Again, the significance of the irimi to take the defender out of the line of the shomen is magnified by the use of swords. The consequences of a failed block are much worse when swords are involved, and it is the body movement rather than the block that ensures the defender's safety. After the defender has blocked the shomen, the attacker instinctively tries to push through the block. The defender uses this pressure to come around for his final cut. Again, the use of swords underlines the foolishness of struggling with a resistant uke. One does not want the outcome of an encounter with swords to be determined by who can push the hardest. The risk is obvious, and so is the importance of responsive movement. This kumiiai could be compared to empty hand shomen ikkyo with a reversal to iriminage in response to resistance by uke (not illustrated). (Uke: Fernando Salazar)

14

Budo: The Original Principle of Aikido

Many were the occasions that I heard Morihei Ueshiba O Sensei, my late teacher, speak on the nature of budo. On one of these, he said,

> I am sure that many of you associate the essence of budo with savage and brute militarism. Nothing could be farther from the truth. In the ancient concept of *kannagara no michi* the ideal of budo is the path of the sage. The word for sage, *hijiri,* literally means "one who understands the spirit." This spirit is the spirit of universal benevolence and is the foundation for establishing world paradise. It is the principle of universal harmony. The Meiji emperor expressed this spirit in the following poem:

> In order to govern the hearts of a million people,
> The first priority is affection.

The Founder of Aikido also used to say, "The way of budo is the way for establishing harmony." O Sensei's interpretation of budo is borne out in many ways, first by the composition of the kanji for the word *bu.* The kanji is made up of the character *hoko* which means "spear" and symbolizes weapons in general, and the character *todomeru,* which means "to stop." Thus *bu* means to stop weapons. While *bu* is often translated into English as "war," its sense is not really the same. As

Budo shingi: The truth of budo

The dictionary definition of *war* is "hostile contention by means of armed forces," while the meaning of *bu,* both literally and in its historical context, encompasses a much broader set of concepts. As the kanji implies, the original intent of bu was to stop war, to protect people from weapons. Budo, or bushido, was the way of the samurai. The word *samurai* means "one who serves." An old proverb expresses well what the true task of the samurai, or bushi, should be: "The samurai is the first to suffer anxiety for human society, and he is the last to seek personal pleasure." The proper attitude of the samurai toward the common people was that of love and concern, such as a father feels toward his children. Samurai were also referred to as yukoku no shi, or noble guardians of the nation. They were the servants of the emperor and the gods, and it was their responsibility to help perpetuate kannagara no michi, the way of the emperor and the gods, in their land. Budo was intended to preserve the orderliness of society, not to promote the use of indiscriminate violence or brute force.

In order to fulfill these functions, a budoka had to be much more than a military technician. It was the samurai class that provided Japan with most of its leaders of society—not just its generals, but its governors, spiritualists, teachers, and other people responsible for the proper management of society. The successful waging of war is only a small part of what it meant to follow the path of budo.

The samurai have continued in this role of management and preservation of society to the present day. It was the members of the samurai class who recognized that the advent of Admiral Perry signaled inevitable change for Japan. While the Tokugawa government clung to its dreams of isolationism, the enlightened among the samurai took steps to

Bu

Yukoku no shi

clung to its dreams of isolationism, the enlightened among the samurai took steps to embrace the new technologies that were being offered. Their actions paved the way for the Meiji Restoration and the rapid industrialization and modernization of Japan. The samurai did not abandon either their traditions or the path of budo but used them for the common good.

The benevolent consciousness of budo also showed itself in the astonishing speed and completeness of the reconstruction of Japan after World War II. The love of their country, their concern for their fellow human beings, their abilities in management and government and their willingness to put aside their own needs as secondary to the good of society as a whole—these were the qualities that allowed the leaders of Japan to rebuild a defeated and war-torn country into a society of great health and economic strength today. In fact, many of Japan's prominent leaders today in both business and government are descended from the ancient samurai families.

Of course, the history of budo is not all a history of benevolence and good government. Budo is a path along a narrow ledge, bordered by precipices. It is easy to fall to one side or the other, either into complacency or aggression. Certainly, many examples of both luxurious corruption and bloody cruelty and violence mar the history of Japan, as they do the history of any society. Budo has its dark side. As the medicines of the doctor make dangerous poisons when misused, the skills of the budoka are capable of causing great havoc and harm. But the ideal and the true goal of budo remain the creation of a strong and benevolent society and the protection of that society's members from harm.

Today, the image of budo is a distorted one, and the word is interpreted in a very limited way. In a Japanese dictionary, one might specific empty hand and weapons training arts, such as karate or kendo. In English, budo is usually defined as meaning martial or military arts. Both definitions lose the larger concept of budo, which makes budo a profound path of study.

Morihei Ueshiba O Sensei said, "Bu is love." His was not an arbitrary or fanciful definition but a considered conclusion based on a lifetime of research, experience, meditation, and labor. Above all, it was a conclusion based on an insight into the workings of life.

Budo is the principle of the center. It knows nothing of the antagonism of opposites. It is a path that requires, first of all, misogi, or "spiritual purification." Budoka must purify their hearts and minds of excessive desire and negative feelings. They must reestablish in their own hearts the true understanding of our divine origin. To become one with God through pure love and devotion in the heart has been the original teaching of budo since ancient times. The highest consciousness of budo, as taught by its greatest masters throughout history, has been the preservation—not the destruction—of life. The goal of budo is for its practitioner to establish the universal spirit in self, society, and country.

Indeed today, the person who follows the path of budo cannot limit the pursuit of benevolence and order and the protection of life to his or her own nation. The world has grown both too large and too small in that through communication and technology we have become an indissolubly connected unit. The actions of any society affect societies around the world. We are a vast global community, but we have the interdependence of a single organism.

The world's present direction must be changed. We cannot continue to solve our differences through argument and war. The

British historian Arnold Toynbee, in his book *Civilization on Trial,* states the dangers of continuing such an approach eloquently and compellingly:

Why cannot civilization go on shambling along, from failure to failure, in the painful, degrading, but not utterly suicidal way in which it has kept going for the first few thousand years of its existence? The answer lies in the recent technological inventions of the modern Western middle class. These gadgets for harnessing the physical forces of non-human nature have left human nature unchanged. The institutions of War and Class are social reflexions of the seamy side of human nature—or what is called original sin—in the kind of society that we call civilization. These social effects of individual human sinfulness have not been abolished by the recent portentous advance in our technological "know-how," but they have not been left unaffected by it either. Not having been abolished, they have been enormously keyed up, like the rest of human life, in respect of their physical potency. Class has now become capable of irrevocably disintegrating Society, and War of annihiliating the entire human race. Evils which hitherto have been merely disgraceful and grievous have now become intolerable and lethal, and, therefore, we in this Westernized world in our generation are confronted with a choice of alternatives which the ruling elements in other societies in the past have always been able to shirk—with dire consequences, invariably, for themselves, but not at the extreme price of bringing to an end the history of mankind on this planet. We are thus confronted with a challenge that our predecessors never had to face: We have to abolish War and Class—and abolish them now—under pain, if we flinch or fail, of seeing them win a victory over man which, this time, would be conclusive and definite.*

* Arnold J. Toynbee, *Civilization on Trial* (New York: Oxford University Press, 1948), pp. 24–25.

This impending crisis is the shared danger of all the developed nations of the world. It is this that makes it so essential to rediscover and return to the original premise of budo, and to cast out the misleading and limited understanding of budo as mere military art. The path of Aikido is the path of budo. This path is one of love, respect, and adoration of the divine principles that infuse this living world and its inhabitants. The mission of the students of budo, the modern samurai, is not the indiscriminate use of military strength but the forging of the world into one family. We must walk on the thin edge of disaster with pure hearts and courage, devoted to this single purpose. The purpose of budo is to foster a spirit of world peace, to protect and nurture humanity. This must be done without bloodshed, without harming others, without taking human life. I wish with all my heart that the people of the world will come to understand the truth of budo.

Once I asked O Sensei, "What is the most important thing for one's training in budo?" His reply was, "The one essential element is the observance in daily life of courtesy and proper etiquette." The courtesy and etiquette that O Sensei spoke of are more than mere politeness. It is more than just not making enemies. *Reigi* ("etiquette" or "decorum"), written with alternative kanji, also means "spirit." Our attitude, and its expression through our actions, shows our real spiritual quality. Those who have difficulty conforming to etiquette will also have difficulty learning the way of the spirit. Unless you have self-respect, proper etiquette will not come easily to you. Courtesy toward others shows your belief in your own spiritual quality. Condescension or rudeness toward others lowers the value of your own character.

The student of budo must learn to be with-

Reigi: normal

out suki. Suki are lapses in consciousness that produce weak points or openings. Failures in etiquette and courtesy toward others are suki, and leave you open to the disregard of other people. I imagine that the relationship between the mentality that allows a person to be without suki in courtesy and the ability to be without suki in self-defense will readily occur to the reader's mind.

Suki also prevents us from fulfilling our responsibilities and from living life fully and deliberately. The greatest masters in all times have always been, and are today, modest and courteous people who live their lives with singleminded purpose. Without the study of this mentality, we lack the most important prerequisite for the mastery of Aikido. Those who have gained a deep understanding of Aikido have all had this attitude in common. In fact, the truly great people in all walks of life, in any society, are all humble and unassuming people. Such people share the ability of introspection and reflection and are people of manners and grace. True character knows nothing of race or nation. Those who practice Aikido must, if they hope to become useful members of society, incorporate these qualities of high human character into themselves.

To change and improve the world we must change and improve ourselves. This is the beginning of budo training. It is the obligation of the student of budo, and of Aikido, to make himself fit to carry on the tradition of budo in a manner consistent with its original meaning. This is the goal and the purpose of your training in Aikido.

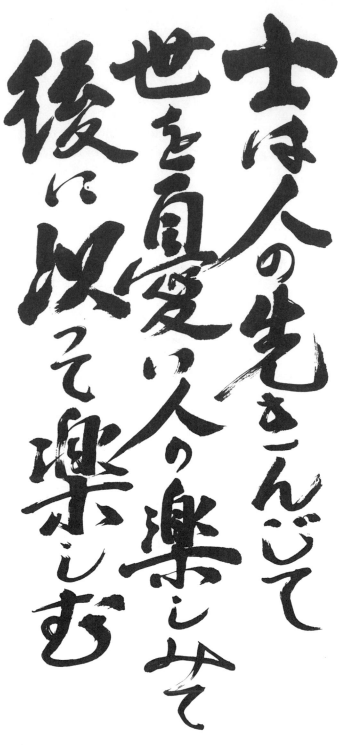

Reigi: spiritual

Shiwa hito no sakiinjite yo-oh urei hito no tanoshimite nochini motute tanoshimu: The samurai is the first to suffer anxiety for human society, and he is the last to seek personal pleasure.

15
The Meaning of Study

Many martial arts schools in the West offer a limited perspective on martial arts training. They present the art that they teach as a purely physical pursuit that has little relation to daily life. The benefits of this kind of study are also limited. Your physical condition may improve, but your character and the quality of your life will not.

I believe that it is much more fruitful to approach budo training as a study that applies to your whole self. In Japan, budo is regarded not as a combat fantasy to be indulged in by the young but as a lifetime study. As a person grows older, the practice may change, but the person can continue to refine ability, spirit, and understanding.

The dojo can be a university of life, a microcosm of the world at large, where you have an opportunity to study many situations and explore the possibilities of interactions with all kinds of people. In my years as an Aikido student and instructor I have met more than forty thousand different people from all walks of life and from many nations and backgrounds. I learned a great deal about life and about human beings not just from my teachers but from all these interesting people. In the course of your training, every person you meet and practice with presents you with a unique opportunity to learn and to grow not just in your Aikido technique but in yourself.

When people come to train at my dojo, I am less concerned with whether they develop excellent technique than with how their training affects the quality of their life. It pleases me when students enjoy their training at the dojo and stay, when they make friends, when their experience with Aikido enriches them.

During the time that I trained with O Sensei, an old man came to the dojo and asked to speak to O Sensei.

"Sensei," he said, "I have worked my whole life running a medical supply company. It has taken all my time. I had no room in my life for anything else. Recently I retired and left the business to my son. Now that I have the time, I'd like to study some of the things I was unable to pursue when I was working. Do you think that it would be possible for me to study Aikido?"

"How old are you?" O Sensei asked.

The man said, "I am over seventy."

O Sensei laughed. "You're younger than I am, then," he said. "I'm over eighty."

"But I'm a beginner," the man protested. "I've never trained in any martial art or even participated in sports. I have no knowledge and no conditioning!"

"Let us say that today I am a beginner too," O Sensei said. "Come, let's practice together."

O Sensei led the man slowly through the basic movements, showing him kokyu tanden ho and gently teaching him how to fall. About two years later that old man, who was so uncertain about his ability to study Aikido, received his black belt.

I'm sure that you can see the point of this

story. It is never too late to learn, to change, and to benefit from new experience. You should not cheat yourself by imposing limits on what you can do by the rigidity of your own mind. Courage, curiosity, and adventurousness, like that of the old man who began his study of Aikido so late in life, can only enhance your world.

That is why the study of ikkyo is so important in Aikido. One moment, one movement decides whether you live or die. You cannot hesitate or waste time, for you have none to waste. You do not get a second chance. It is as important to keep this attitude in your life as it is in your training. In training you sharpen yourself by treating each encounter as a one-time event, a single chance. In your life, embrace each moment and make it count. There is wisdom to be found under the blade of the sword.

Budo can help teach you to manage your life and to govern yourself. It takes confidence, awareness, receptiveness, and self-control to accomplish ikkyo. All these qualities are of value in any situation. The skills that you learn in Aikido training can be applied to enhance your other endeavors. Budo teaches you to depend on yourself, rather than allowing yourself to be a victim of your circumstances. The richness or poverty of your own life is your own responsibility.

If you accept the idea that budo is a study that can encompass all aspects of your life, there is another fallacy which you must avoid. This is the temptation to turn the teachings of your art into doctrines, or your teacher into an idol. We have all seen cases in which religions turn into cults, or in which the adherents of a religion become so rigid in their interpretation of its teaching that they leave no room for thought or charity in their prac-

tice of the religion. We have also seen various people gain power over a group of followers and lead them to commit dangerous and destructive acts. We read of many occasions throughout history in which a teaching of great benevolence and wisdom was distorted and used to ill purpose.

Budo, while not a religion, is prey to some of the same dangers and distortions. A valid lesson can be used as an excuse to justify selfish, arrogant behavior. This is one of the reasons why in Japan people are judged not by their beliefs but by their behavior. It is not which training you follow that is important but how you put that training to use.

I feel it is important to keep your teacher's role in your training in perspective. Your teacher is a guide, not a guru. There is a great difference between respect and idolization. Ultimately, you are responsible for your own life and your own training. Your teacher can help you and offer you suggestions but cannot change your life. That is up to you. Your teacher cannot be a perfect master. Like any human being your teacher will be full of faults. Your obligation as a student is to take what your teacher offers that is of value, to integrate it into yourself, and to improve on it. Between teacher and student there should be no competition. The student should not nurture unrealistic expectations and then fault the teacher for not living up to them. The greatest tribute that you can pay to a teacher is to surpass him in the quality of your life and your practice.

Aikido teaches a simple secret: the development of better life is dependent on bettering yourself. Aikido offers no miracles except the miracle of your own existence and your human potential. Remember that you are a part of the universe. To ruin your life or to waste it is to ruin a piece of the universe. With your birth you hold the key that opens the door to heaven. The most important duty in each person's life is to use that key and to make his or her life a manifestation of the heaven that it lies within our power to create.

16
Aikido as Explained by the Founder and Doshu

The Founder's son, Aiki Doshu Kisshomaru Ueshiba, has written:

Aikido, founded by the late Morihei Ueshiba, has its origins in many different styles of ancient bujutsu. Ueshiba O Sensei refined these techniques and, through his own research into the human character, added spiritual elements which distinguish them from those of other martial ways. The way of fighting took a quantum leap to become a complete spiritual path equal to any of those left to us by the sages of ancient times.

Aikido is a modern and original form of budo based on the conviction of Ueshiba O Sensei that "through constant unremitting training of the mind and body, the way of humanity can be realized." Since its original form, certain necessary and reasonable adjustments have been made in order to pass Aikido down to the general public successfully, yet its main emphasis remains unchanged. This premise is that true budo does not nurture an irrational or forceful attitude. It does not involve competition or comparison of each other's relative ability. Rather, it is a way of purifying one's own character.

Aikido, depending on the actual realization of this experience, has the ultimate goal of unifying one's life energy (ki) with that of the infinite universe. The budo known as Aikido is a harmonious blending of ki with reason, the universal principle by which it is governed.

In the course of forming Aikido, Ueshiba O Sensei underwent many different kinds of training. In the years before World War II, he studied Kito ryu jujutsu, Yagyu ryu jujutsu, Shin Kage ryu kenjutsu and Daito ryu jujutsu, to mention just a few. He also studied the ancient texts of Japanese religious doctrines and became well versed in ancient writings and lectures. The combination of these spiritual researches and the various bujutsu bore a unique fruit. One confronts one's opponent bare-handed and, at the same time, controls his ki and defeats him. This is a living form of Japanese budo that, having been refined and polished, meets the rational needs of this modern day.

Aiki no Kurai

If we look at records of military strategy and at the secret teachings of ancient budo, the word aiki represents the deepest, most advanced lesson—winning without fighting. Aiki is formless, timeless, and void. It is one with the divine spirit of the universe and of nature. Like a crystal mirror it reflects all things as they are. When the heart is pure and bright, no one can become your enemy. Each person, as a living being, contains, and is contained within, the infinite whole. If we be-

Aiki Doshu Kisshomaru Ueshiba

come one with the universe, we will become the embodiment of michi, the way. The true world of aiki exists beyond form and technique. It is an abstract and difficult concept to grasp. It is a state of consciousness free of pettiness and selfishness, in which one is at peace with oneself and the world. To reach this state of mind must be your intent if you wish to draw closer to the reality of Aikido.

When your life becomes a clear mirror, without distortions, you will become one not only with your practice partners but also with the laws of nature. This is called aiki no kurai, the highest consciousness of aiki. O Sensei once said to me,

> Saotome, if you wish to understand *aiki no kurai,* study the world of nature. Think of how an eagle, flying high in the sky, is able to catch

fish which swim beneath the water's surface. From the shore, where we must stand, the current of the ocean distorts our view; yet from high aloft the eagle sees the fish, indeed, the shadows of the fish, as if they were reflected in a mirror. The eagle plucks the fish from the water as easily as we might pick up a stone on an open plain. Likewise, the eagle cannot match the swift-footed rabbit on the ground, but from the sky he easily follows the rabbit's course. *Aiki no kurai* is not only a teaching of the martial arts, but a lesson of nature itself. Nature is also our dojo. The intricate variations of the seasons, the beauty of the flowers in the field are our teachers, and they lead us to the highest consciousness of aiki. Any serious student of Aikido must observe the phenomena of the universe in motion to find the meaning of their study. As you come to understand these phenomena, you must apply your understanding to your practice of budo. This is my teaching.

I also remember an occasion on which O Sensei lectured to a religious group. O Sensei said,

> The demonstration of Aikido that I just gave to you may have given you the impression of an old man playing with children. There is much truth in this impression. Unless you bring a sense of pleasure and of fun to your Aikido practice, the truth of Aikido is difficult to attain. I take great pleasure in my pursuit of the path of the gods. Aikido must be a dance of the gods. Remember the myth of "Ama no iwata biraki," the opening of the rock door of heaven. In this ancient story Amaterasu Omi Kami, the sun goddess, hid herself in a cave and sealed it with a door of stone, and the whole world became veiled in darkness. In order to bring light back to the world the other gods devised a plan. They staged a dancing drama in front of the door to Amaterasu's cave. As they danced and celebrated, the sounds of their laughter and enjoyment reached the goddess's ears, and she opened the door a tiny way, curious to see what revels were going on outside her cave. At that moment, Teji Kara no Mikoto, the god of in-

Aiki no kurai

comparable strength, pushed open the rock door and led Amaterasu back out into the world, and the world was once again filled with her light. This old story provides a lesson concerning the duty of budo. Just as the strong god brought Amaterasu's light back into the world, budoka must work to create a paradise on this earth, to bring light to the world's people. This is the true purpose of budo. Just as you, who follow the teachings of your religion, all pray for peace and human happiness, the Aikido of Ueshiba works for precisely the same goal. In the eyes of God all of humanity is one family.

The young students who participated in this demonstration with me are *shihan-dai*. I send them to teach at universities and military academies. When they venture out on their own, they will become great teachers and aikidoka. Yet even then they will have far to go to master the real depths of their study. I myself am still a stu-

dent of the way. The wisdom and the laws of God are immeasurable and unfathomably deep.

You might ask what is the most important thing in Aikido training. It is to look at yourself, your innermost soul. The reality of your own life must surely lead you back to its origins, to the beginning of the universe. If you succeed in doing this, you will intuitively realize that your past, present and future, already integral parts of your being, are manifestations of the divine will and the love of God. Each of the individual cells of your body carries a map of the divine plan of creation. Because of this we can realize directly the great love of the creator. Universal consciousness is our birthright. We must go beyond all antagonism and disunity. This is what constitutes *aiki no kurai*.

I would like to show you the *kotodama* of Aikido and the *kagura mai,* the dance of the gods as they stand on the floating bridge of heaven. It has been a long time since I performed this *kagura mai*. When performed with the spear, it symbolizes the working of the creative energy of the universe. It portrays the divine inspiration of the *Kojiki,* the legends of origin of Japanese mythology. It is the scientific laws of the universe represented through bu. The secret toward which this old man is training himself is the way to open the rock door that shuts the light away from the human mind. It is to change the world of war and ignorance into a world of divine light. It is to improve the spiritual quality of all human beings and to open their intuitive consciousness. This is the purpose of the original bu, which has been reborn as Aikido. That is why I call Aikido the budo of love. It is receiving the spirit of God.

Neither budo nor religion seeks only individual salvation. Their higher mission is the search for peace and harmony for the whole human race. Reading prayers and scriptures does not suffice. We must express this consciousness through our actions. This is the spirit and the intent of budo. The path must be of universal love for all sentient beings. Science has already produced enough weapons to destroy the whole world, yet the science of the spirit is miserably underdeveloped. As a result uneasiness and fear are omnipresent in modern society. But aiki is also omnipresent, and it is eternal; it is the function of life energy itself. Aikido was born of a deep wish to realize the unity of humankind and to tap the power of the harmony of creation and the true nature of the human spirit.

O Sensei's vision in creating Aikido obviously went far beyond creating a new way of movement and of doing technique. I hope that the readers of this book will take the time to study and absorb O Sensei's words, and that they will keep them in mind as they engage in their daily training.

17

Mirror of the Spirit: The Aikido Dojo

Geography without question influences the way that a nation's culture develops. In the United States the seemingly limitless amount of land and the varied climates and terrains fostered a culture that prizes individualism and innovation. The veneration of the adventurous and pioneering spirit is one of the strongest common bonds among the people of the contemporary United States, a country that has evolved into a nation of almost chaotic heterogeneity. On the other hand, not only has Japan throughout its history had a fairly small geographical area to accommodate a large population, but it is also a nation composed of islands. People were—and are—forced into close association with one another with few avenues for escape. Japanese culture has consequently evolved as one that venerates order, conformity, and law. The welfare of the group is considered more important than the welfare of the individual. Even the fairly conservative American is distrustful of authority and alert to any power that threatens his liberty. The average Japanese sees authority as necessary to the survival of society, and obedience to authority as a form of cooperation rather than coercion. Certainly, there is consensus and conformity in the United States and individualism in Japan, but the priorities of the respective countries remain clearly different.

Understanding the concept of submission to authority and to the needs of the community as an act of consent rather than capitulation is vital to understanding the Japanese character. This concept is also important to understanding the meaning and worth of the Japanese institution of the dojo, and particularly the Aikido dojo.

The word *dojo* means "place of the way." Originally dojo were adjuncts to temples and religious groups. They were places in which monks and other religious persons were trained in the disciplines and practices of their faith. Eventually, the name *dojo* came to apply to places where various other nonreligious disciplines were studied—swordsmanship, calligraphy, dance, and other pursuits demanding rigorous training. Given the inclination in Japanese society at large for embracing rule and order, it is not surprising that the Japanese adopted the model of monastic discipline as the pattern for schools to train people in secular arts. Also, the ancient Japanese religion of Shinto, which is largely responsible for forming the Japanese attitude toward religion, did not have a concept of an external God imposing his will on man and nature but saw all things in nature as having a spark of the divine. The separation between religious and secular pursuits was thus not as sharply defined in Japan as it is in the West, nor did religion in Japan tend as much to exclude a variety of ideas. The concept of *do,* or a way of life to which one gave one's whole being, came to apply to any important vocation pursued with dedication.

Another great contributing influence in the modern martial arts dojo is the ethic of warrior societies. These, I think, are similar throughout the world, due to the common demands that war places upon soldiers. In order to make people fit to face the supreme stress of combat intense discipline is necessary. All armies and warrior societies enforce codes that brook no rebellion. The most successful of such groups are the ones whose members support the system through their belief in its importance and in the goals for which they fight. Warrior societies in which coercion is applied on unwilling members are rarely stable, productive, or useful.

It almost seems unnecessary to add that courtesy and strict rules of etiquette were required in all dojo, regardless of the discipline they taught. Any enclosed society becomes intolerable without courtesy and consideration for one's fellow members. Formal rules of etiquette help keep one's behavior in order when one's temper gets frayed. In the martial arts dojo, the influence of warriors' special conditions introduces an additional inducement to courteous and chivalrous behavior. The consequences of a discourteous act could be death rather than mere discord. This is one of the reasons that warrior societies in any nation put such a high value on courtesy and chivalry.

Since Aikido is a martial art whose purpose is the refinement of the human spirit and the promotion of peace in the world, the Aikido dojo includes the influences of both the warrior societies and the religious dojo. Aikido is not a religion, for it has no dogma or doctrine, but it is a deeply spiritual pursuit. The Aikido dojo is a temple of the spirit, both that of the individual human being and the divine spirit that imbues all things in the universe. The Aikido dojo must also maintain the severity and discipline of a community of warriors, for Aikido is budo, the way of the warrior. Aikido is not meant to be an abstract theory of spiritual values, but a practical training that strengthens your courage, your internal serenity, and your ability to relate to others. It is meant to change your mental attitude so that you do not revert to aggression and violence under stress but instead continue to behave in a fashion that prevents or stops conflict. Aikido is meant to give you the courage of your convictions.

The essential elements of the dojo are commitment, cooperation, discipline, order, courtesy, and a faith in the goal toward which the members of the dojo are striving. How do these elements manifest themselves practically? First, the students in the dojo must share in the responsibility for the running and maintenance of the dojo. The Aikido dojo must be a cooperative organization in which all members are concerned with the welfare of the dojo and each other. The dojo is not a gymnasium where hired help take care of its needs. Students at a dojo must look at cleaning the dojo as a spiritual exercise; the state of the dojo is the reflection of the internal state of its students.

Maintaining personal cleanliness is an act of consideration and respect for yourself, for your fellow students, and for the art of Aikido. The Aikido student must keep his training clothes and weapons clean and in good repair. He must not leave his belongings strewn around but must keep them neatly stored. He should be aware of the whereabouts of his weapons at all times.

While cooperation is important, the dojo is not a democracy. From your sensei on down through the hierarchy of senior students (*sempai*) and junior students (*kohai*), there must be a chain of obedience and humility strengthened by mutual respect. Senior students must provide a good example to their juniors and must support and reinforce their sensei's teachings. Especially in a large dojo, it is impossible for the sensei to see to the complete instruction of all students personally. It is the responsibility of the senior students to make sure that their juniors are properly taught and that the necessary work of the dojo gets done. Junior students must respect their senior students and not argue or resist instruction. New students come not knowing the ways of the dojo or the essential principles of Aikido. In order for them to learn, they must remain open-minded and humble. Senior students, on the other hand, must behave in a way to merit respect and must not use their position to humiliate* or behave arrogantly toward their juniors. The hierarchy of the dojo in no way denies the basic respect that you should show all your fellow human beings. Good technique does not excuse immature and petty behavior. Without good manners the dojo turns into a jungle, and what was meant to be the pursuit of spiritual improvement becomes a dangerous training.

In your personal observance of the rules of etiquette, it is important to maintain decorum and to exhibit a disciplined and attractive demeanor. You should strictly adhere to the forms of courtesy and should be neat and correct in your dress and attitude. To get on the mat incompletely or improperly dressed, to lounge around on the mat in a sloppy or informal manner—these external improprieties are signs of mental and spiritual laxness. Maintaining proper decorum, conversely, strengthens your internal orderliness.

Thus the dojo's etiquette and rules are not empty formalities but rather serve to create conditions essential to good training. In the modern Aikido dojo, for example, students are expected to have their own weapons for training. To borrow anyone else's weapons without permission is a terrible breach of etiquette. To understand the reason for this you only have to think about warriors who actually fight for their lives. For these people, their lives depend not only on their skill but on the quality and condition of their weapons and their ability to lay their hands on them at any time. It is not difficult to see why touching or taking another person's weapon without permission was a killing matter in the warrior cultures of the past. A person who committed such a careless and inconsiderate act was not likely to get a chance to mend his ways.

In the Aikido dojo we do not wish to train killers, nor are breaches of etiquette punished by death. Yet if you forget or completely ignore the mortal seriousness behind martial arts training and the protection against deadly accident that etiquette was designed to provide, I believe your training will lose depth and your understanding will be limited. The awareness that life and death are the issues at stake in budo increases your appreciation of the meaning of both. Your sense of the value of not only your own life but the lives of your fellow human beings will become much greater.

18

Lectures by O Sensei

The Importance of Learning

"First you must gain insight into the natural world. You must learn to see the depths of its reality. If you glance casually over the things of this life, their real significance eludes you.

"I want my students to observe all of life's phenomena. This includes listening to people, taking what is valuable from what they do and say and making it your own. All of this is raw material for your reflection and your inspiration. It can begin to open your soul. Paying attention to the realities of this world will lead you to fresh insights. If you make use of these insights in your daily life and contemplate the results, your life will become more orderly. Step by step you will raise your spiritual level. Persevering in this kind of honest and open-minded examination of yourself and the world will eventually enable you to grasp the divine wisdom and supreme consciousness that inhabit the material world. I want my students to accept life in all its forms as their teacher. If they succeed in doing this, they will grow in both depth and purity. The vital energy of nature is the greatest teacher of all.

"Examine the orderly cycles of the sun, moon, and stars, the gradual change of the seasons, the flow of a river through an open valley, or the graceful movement of water as it rushes between rocks. You can learn to see parallel movements within your own body as well. You will also gain knowledge and progress toward true understanding by reading ancient texts and studying the many wonderful interpretations of them by teachers past and present. You must then translate the insights that you gain into your daily life and practice them through the way of bu. As you experience things on an increasingly deeper level, you must continually reexamine the truth of your understanding of reality and nature. Both the written and the spoken word will help you toward this goal. It is the task of the budoka to make what he learns new and to make it an integral part of himself. The student of budo cannot afford to overlook the fine arts or the sciences. Knowledge surrounds us in an infinite variety of forms. Do not slight any of them or take any of them lightly.

"There is nothing in this world that cannot teach us. Some people, for example, will shy away from the teachings of religion. This is evidence that they have not grasped the deeper meanings of these teachings. Religious teachings contain much insight and wisdom. You must understand this and express your understanding through budo.

"In my younger days, I became a convert of a certain religion, and in one of its songs I discovered a phrase concerning "the plum flower that blossoms once in three spiritual

Do: The Way

Kannagara no michi

worlds." First, the five petals of the plum blossom represent the five forms of universal energy: earth, water, fire, wind, and sky. If you think of the plum blossom in this way, you will discover in this phrase a lesson about the universe itself. You can see the plum blossom as an actual manifestation of the universal spirit. Also, in the way that the plum blossom opens only once and never again you can see the reflection of the unique beginning of creation. Looked at differently, the opening of the plum blossom represents the opening of the rock door of heaven told of in Japanese mythology. [See chapter 16 for a full explanation of this myth.]

"This world is actually a complete manifestation of Heaven and Earth. We, as human beings created in the same divine, universal image, must make this earth into a truly heavenly place. We must complete and perfect human society. It is important that the people who train themselves in budo encompass the universe within themselves. The mission of

Aikido is to achieve this harmony with the universe. To accomplish this must become your whole mind and heart."

The Purpose of Aikido

"I wonder if you grasp the real purpose of Aikido? It is not merely training yourself in the techniques of bujutsu. Its other purpose is the creation of a world of beauty, grace, and elegance. It is to make this world a better place, a world of joy. As I am always saying, God gave us this world, and the world is all one family. We have the continued privilege of enjoying its beauty and splendor. It is our obligation, as human beings, to establish a society that does justice to that beauty and splendor. Our goal in budo is not merely to protect ourselves. We must accept the gift of

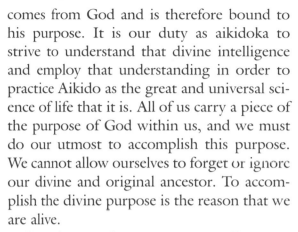

Misogi: Spiritual purification

the divine love of God and constantly strive to honor that gift by nurturing the changes that will bring happiness to the world. If we truly honor the sacred heart of budo, we must work for peace, for a world without quarrels, without misery, without conflict. This is the real reason that we practice Aikido. Aikido is a way of making the universal principle clear. Its purpose is to create a reasonable and logical world. The society that harmoniously combines body and mind produces a world of unity. We ourselves must take the responsibility to realize the heart and mind of God.

"We cannot place exclusive importance on either the material or the spiritual world. In reality they are one and the same thing. The modern age has witnessed great progress in the physical sciences, but the science of the soul and spirit lags very far behind. The development of the spirit is not only a very important part of the true mission of science. It is the inescapable responsibility imposed on us by our very existence, an existence that comes from God and is therefore bound to his purpose. It is our duty as aikidoka to strive to understand that divine intelligence and employ that understanding in order to practice Aikido as the great and universal science of life that it is. All of us carry a piece of the purpose of God within us, and we must do our utmost to accomplish this purpose. We cannot allow ourselves to forget or ignore our divine and original ancestor. To accomplish the divine purpose is the reason that we are alive.

"In other words, we must never allow ourselves to forget the concept of chushin, our center. All things are controlled by the stability and the quality of their center, the place where their being is born. We may call this place the life force, or kannagara, the universal flow of divine consciousness. Whatever you wish to call it, it is the force that comes from our hara. The only "original" sin is to lose this connection with our *origin* and to be oblivious to the great gift of our life. To forget your true nature is the beginning of a greedy attachment to life, which is the beginning of sin. This is the root of all chaos in modern society. Our life, as human beings, is blessed even beyond that of other forms of life. If you do not acknowledge this, you force disorder and chaos upon nature. We must not forget our obligation as human beings. That obligation is to create the paradise that is this world's true form.

"Once we are truly aware of the universal plan and its divine purpose, we no longer have any real choice but to apprentice ourselves to the service of this most superb and sacred endeavor. This is the essence and heart of budo, and it is the principle aim of Aikido. When we become aware that our life is a gift from the divine consciousness of the infinite

O Sensei Morihei Ueshiba

disappears. We no longer see inside and outside as two entities but as parts of a whole. They serve the same function, and work for the same ultimate purpose. The infinite universe and the way of Aiki are the light that signals the dawn of the consciousness of human beings."

O Sensei's last Kagami Biraki with Mitsugi Saotome taking ukemi (Photograph courtesy of Aiki News)

universe, we come to realize our true nature as children of God. We were born on this earth so that the great task of our creator might be fulfilled. To work for its accomplishment is our own greatest fulfillment as well.

"In Japan, the feeling of shame is regarded as a certain kind of sensitivity and, therefore, a virtue. How can we not feel shame if we ignore our divine nature and our true purpose in life? This is the origin of all shame. Real understanding of Aikido will only come about through daily purification (*misogi*) and through constantly striving for the creation of a better world. Where a center exists, it implies all that surrounds it.

"If our center is strong, however, the distinction between the center and its periphery

19

The Hakama
and Its Meaning

When I was uchi deshi to O Sensei, everyone was required to wear a hakama for practice, beginning with the first time they stepped on the mat. There were no restrictions on the type of hakama you could wear then, so the dojo was a very colorful place. One saw hakama of all sorts, all colors and all qualities, from kendo hakama, to the striped hakama used in Japanese dance, to the costly silk hakama called sendai-hira. I imagine that some beginning student caught the devil for borrowing his grandfather's expensive hakama, meant to be worn only for special occasions and ceremonies, and wearing out its knees in suwariwaza practice.

I vividly remember the day that I forgot my hakama. I was preparing to step on the mat for practice, wearing only my dogi, when O Sensei stopped me.

"Where is your hakama?" he demanded sternly. "What makes you think you can receive your teacher's instruction wearing nothing but your underwear? Have you no sense of propriety? You are obviously lacking the attitude and the etiquette necessary in one who pursues budo training. Go sit on the side and watch class!"

This was only the first of many scoldings I was to receive from O Sensei. However, my ignorance on this occasion prompted O Sensei to lecture his uchi deshi after class on the meaning of the hakama. He told us that the hakama was traditional garb for ko-budo students and asked if any of us knew the reason for the seven pleats in the hakama.

"They symbolize the seven virtues of budo," O Sensei said. "These are *jin* (benevolence), *gi* (honor or justice), *rei* (courtesy and etiquette), *chi* (wisdom, intelligence), *shin* (sincerity), *chu* (loyalty), and *koh* (piety). We find these qualities in the distinguished samurai of the past. The hakama prompts us to reflect on the nature of true bushido. Wearing it symbolizes traditions that have been passed down to us from generation to generation. Aikido is born of the bushido spirit of Japan, and in our practice we must strive to polish the seven traditional virtues."

Currently, most Aikido dojo do not follow O Sensei's strict policy about wearing the hakama. Its meaning has degenerated from a symbol of traditional virtue to that of a status symbol for yudansha. I have traveled to many dojo in many nations. In many of the places where only the yudansha wear hakama, the yudansha have lost their humility. They think of the hakama as a prize for display, as the visible symbol of their superiority. This type of attitude makes the ceremony of bowing to O Sensei, with which we begin and end each class, a mockery of his memory and his art.

Worse still, in some dojo, women of kyu rank (and only the women) are required to wear hakama, supposedly to preserve their modesty. To me this is insulting and discriminatory to women aikidoka. It is also insulting to male aikidoka, for it assumes a low-mindedness on their part that has no place on the Aikido mat.

To see the hakama put to such petty use saddens me. It may seem a trivial issue to some people, but I remember very well the great importance that O Sensei placed on wearing hakama. I cannot dismiss the significance of this garment, and no one, I think, can dispute the great value of the virtues it symbolizes. In my dojo and its associated schools I encourage all students to wear hakama regardless of their rank or grade. (I do not require it before they have achieved their first grading, since beginners in the United States do not generally have Japanese grandfathers whose hakama they can borrow.) I feel that wearing the hakama and knowing its meaning, helps students to be aware of the spirit of O Sensei and keep alive his vision.

If we can allow the importance of the hakama to fade, perhaps we will begin to allow things fundamental to the spirit of Aikido to slip into oblivion as well. If, on the other hand, we are faithful to O Sensei's wishes regarding our practice dress, our spirits may be more faithful to the dream to which he dedicated his life.

20

Beginning the Journey toward Awakened Consciousness

On 7 April 1964, I had an experience that changed my life. I have never spoken publicly about it, for O Sensci advised me, in a confidential talk, that I should keep it to myself. He felt that my experience might be misunderstood and my motives for revealing it misjudged. My own sense of reserve concerning this experience was so great that it bordered on embarrassment, and on the occasions on which I felt moved to write about it my own feelings combined with O Sensei's admonitions to prevent me from doing so.

I now feel, however, that the time has come to communicate my experience to my fellow followers of the way of Aikido, for I regard this incident as the dawn of my awakened consciousness. I do this not to boast of my own enlightenment or wave my own banner but to share with others my understanding of the possibilities and the reality of what O Sensei meant when he spoke of connection between oneself and all things in the universe.

Before the fateful day in April my greatest personal problem was an overriding dislike of myself. Looking back now at my disposition when I was young, I have to admit that

some of that dislike was merited. I was constantly aggressive, contentious, and competitive. I behaved this way from the time that I was a child. Constantly scarred from fighting with my schoolmates. I was a source of trouble and concern to both my parents and teachers. I was always looking for challenge and adventure.

My original purpose for studying Aikido was more to continue the training I had begun with judo and jujutsu than to seek enlightenment or to improve my character. Indeed, I wanted little more than to become very strong. I still retained my childhood visions of living the life of bushido. Toward this end, I trained in Aikido six to nine hours a day.

It is a testimony to the effectiveness of Aikido training in improving human beings that my training began to change me despite my aggressive intent. I began to channel some of the energy I had previously expended on seeking conflict toward introspection and contemplation. I feel very fortunate in the inspired instruction that I received from several great teachers, especially that which I received from Morihei Ueshiba O Sensei. It

Hatsu O Oku sama (the Founder's wife), Mitsugi Saotome, and other students with the Founder

was a great honor and privilege and an invaluable treasure of my life to have lived for a time at his side. Without the aid of O Sensei and others I do not know if I would have been able to find my way out of the maze of self-hatred and aggression that imprisoned me.

As I continued my training, my dissatisfaction with myself increased to the point where it tormented me. I couldn't decide whether to live or die. To continue to improve myself seemed an enterprise of questionable worth. In the depths of this despairing state of mind, about a week before the experience that changed my life, I lost my appetite completely. I simply sat in seiza, going for long periods of time without food or sleep. During this time I frequently practiced shin kokyu deep breathing, the chin kon ki shin practice taught to me by O Sensei. I did this not with the intention of seeking enlightenment but only to find some peace of mind and a release from my own torment. By the end of this week I was in a state of exhaustion. The sound of my own breathing echoing in a vast emptiness became the reality of my existence.

As I sat in seiza practicing shin kokyu in the small hours of the morning of 7 April 1964, I heard the clock strike four. The deep tones of the chime felt as if they were resonating inside me. The sound vibrated in my body painfully, traveling through my neck and exploding in my head. I began to shake violently and everything became dark. All the strength went out of my body. My hips became very hot and I experienced a sensation like fire ascending from the base of my spine to the top of my head. Then it seemed as if the fire passed through the top of my head and expanded through the room. It appeared as if the very air were made of golden light or a rain of golden mist. I felt at that moment as if I were dying. I fell forward onto my face and lost consciousness altogether.

I don't know how long I lay unconscious. Some sounds brought my awareness trickling back to me like a clear spring seeping to the surface from deep under the earth. I do not know what to call this experience—an illusion, a religious experience, a strange psychological phenomenon? I cannot say. It was certainly a very mysterious occurrence.

Whatever it was that happened to me, it produced a profound change in my state of mind. My body felt light and my spirit joyous. My former feelings of suffering and an uncontrollable belligerence had left me. In fact, I experienced my former suffering as proof of my being alive and realized that to be alive was a value beyond any pain. I felt the force of life flowing like a current between myself and my surroundings as if I and all else shared one universal source of energy. As time went on, I found that this change in my consciousness was permanent and had altered my character. My feelings of hatred and envy toward others vanished. In their place I felt joy, openness, optimism, and gratitude for life. In my Aikido practice I lost the need to compare my abilities with those of others. I realized the freedom from attachment that comes with the recognition that human life—indeed the universe of life—begins and ends with mu, the eternal void.

When I attended class the morning after this experience, I was amazed. My techniques felt smooth and effortless. It seemed as if my partners were moving in slow motion. Many people in the dojo said to me, "I don't know what it is, Saotome, but you seem like a different person today." Before this time, I had enjoyed practicing violently; now I became interested in exploring Aikido techniques. Competition ceased to interest me. Its worthlessness became apparent.

After the class, O Sensei called me into his room. I wondered whether, as usual, I had done something wrong. When I entered O Sensei's room, he asked me to sit down and to prepare with him to make a prayer to the gods. He told me that if I had been able to grasp the true meaning of being reborn, I would come, in time, to understand the true meaning of budo. He said, "Oneness is simply that—oneness. All things in creation are linked and interdependent. Beyond time and space they echo together in waves of the spirit and in doing so confirm each other's existence. Aikido must manifest this living and divine principle of the universe. It must be beyond the sphere of ideology and philosophy. Aikido is the path of direct realization of the universal spirit through actual practice. It is the totality of the body and the spirit together. The patterns of Aikido exist deep within our subconscious and are the patterns of the divine reflections of life." O Sensei paused. Then he said, "Well, that's enough of

Chin kon ki shin

your listening to this old man's speech. Let us pray for your rebirth."

O Sensei began a Shinto prayer, "Taka ama hara ni," which he was accustomed to say on the occasions when he felt that one of his students had achieved enlightenment. As I heard the prayer, I realized that O Sensei had understood what I had experienced, though he did not say so directly. As I sat beside him, the fire of the candle that he had been burning blurred as the tears filled my eyes. When O Sensei finished praying, he turned to me and said, "From this time on your training will progress through many levels. Keep what happened to yourself for now. Many people have a distaste for anything that seems like a religious experience. Yet if people would recognize it, the world of satori is within us all. Our life force, the basis of our humanity, is accessible to everyone."

21

Aikido: Finding Its Future in Its Past

There is an ancient proverb in Japan: "Seek the past if you would learn the future." Studying history improves your understanding of present values and causes you to reflect on your own experiences and actions and see their meaning in the greater context of humanity's experience. Your way becomes more clear and your missteps grow fewer. You face the future with a greater sense of reality and therefore a greater ability to approach it creatively. This is the sense behind the word keiko, or daily practice. At this point in the development of Aikido, I feel that it is important to apply the wisdom of this ancient proverb to the future of Aikido, of its continuance and growth.

Among modern Japanese budoka, Morihei Ueshiba is considered a genius and master the equal of the renowned Miyamoto Musashi. If it had not been for Ueshiba O Sensei's life of rigorous training and superhuman effort in his search for his own spiritual awakening and for the way, Aikido as we know it would never have developed. The history of Aikido begins with Morihei Ueshiba. His prayers for world peace led him to create the "way of harmony." He elevated the killing techniques of battle into a method of purifying human beings so that they might harmoniously co-exist and prosper.

Morihei Ueshiba O Sensei always kept the realities of the world in mind. He did not dream of a fictitious utopia. His life was dedicated to the needs of the real world. Both his personal experience and his clear vision gave him deep understanding of the terrible and devastating effect that two world wars had had on mankind. He knew that his own personal meditations on peace and his heartfelt wish for peace had their reflections in the world at large, a world transformed by the experience of global war.

Aikido, as O Sensei conceived and created it, is a *practical* philosophy to help the world. It is a physical expression of the original meaning expressed by the character *bu* (see chapter 14). This meaning has been preserved in the kanji and reminds us of the true meaning of the word, however its sense may have been distorted in the centuries of its use. O Sensei's approach toward self-defense was meant to be a way to teach the defense of the world. The wisdom and strategy of self-defense, evolved through the labors of generations of warriors and realized and redefined by O Sensei, is the purpose of study, not personal self-defense. O Sensei constantly refined Aikido training as a way to reform your whole being, your spirit, your body, and your relation to the spirit of the universe. Aikido arms the spirit, strengthening it so it may pursue budo, the way of ending war.

The spirit of Aikido has soared above the walls that humans have built to protect their differences and has spread throughout the world. Its worldwide appeal confirms Aikido's universal properties. For many, Aikido touches the wellspring of life, as was O Sensei's intent. Aikido provides a truth sought after—and not found—by the physical sciences and by various modern philosophies, religions, and other forms of modern education. It provides a way to explore the principles of the universe and experience them in our own bodies. All this was Morihei Ueshiba O Sensei's creation and his gift to the world.

Here, I would like to make a point about the originality of O Sensei's creation and the uniqueness of Aikido. As Aikido has become more widely known, it has attracted the interest of intelligent people in every discipline. Some have been led by their interest to delve into the history of Japan, of bujutsu, famous samurai, and the martial arts of ancient China. Some of these people have drawn erroneous conclusions about the origins of Aikido. They say that it is nothing new, that the techniques of Aikido were created and used in other martial arts long ago.

These critics have totally missed the point. To make such an assertion is like claiming that because the automobile is descended from the horse-drawn cart, there is no difference between the two. As far as I know, no one has made such an absurd claim. Everyone recognizes the immense conceptual progress and the achievement in technology that separate the two.

The inventor of the wheel and the inventor of the cart that efficiently used the wheel were no less geniuses than the inventor of the gasoline-powered engine. All are achievements to be admired in their own right. Yet each represents a separate achievement, worthy of distinction. So, too, with the various martial arts, both ancient and modern. To deny the worth of the ancient martial arts' creativity or to deny the originality of their successors is to be blind to the evolution of the disciplines. To put other martial arts into the same category as Aikido is to diminish the value of both. Each should be considered for its own relative value and its own contribution to modern society, as one would consider the jet engine of a plane and the gasoline-powered engine of a car as inventions of equal value.

Obviously, O Sensei did not create Aikido in a vacuum. His training in other martial arts was extensive. He studied the arts of sword, jo, spear, and jujutsu, among many others. His knowledge of history, too, was profound. It is also true that techniques from other arts—some of them very ancient—form the basis for many Aikido techniques. I have no wish to deny the contributions other arts have made to Aikido nor to withhold the respect that is their due. But Aikido is the unique creation of Morihei Ueshiba. To observe the resemblance between the techniques of Aikijutsu and Aikido is one thing. To see the purpose behind the techniques is another. You must look below the surface to see their true meaning. Soy sauce and Coca Cola look very much the same, but to use the first to quench thirst or the latter to flavor a dish would produce disastrous results. A knife used in the kitchen for the preparation of food is a tool of creativity, but the same knife may be used for murderous assault. O Sensei's transformation of a martial art from something limited to personal self-defense to an art dedicated to elevating the human con-

Wago: Harmony

Chusei: Loyalty

sciousness toward the defense of humanity is his creation alone.

Morihei Ueshiba's role as the creator of Aikido is undeniable and his dedication and personal magnetism will long be remembered. There are, however, others who played important roles in introducing Aikido to the general public and assuring its popular acceptance. Chief among these people is Kisshomaru Ueshiba, O Sensei's son and the current doshu. For one thing, O Sensei was very reluctant to make Aikido teaching available to the general public. It was Doshu who convinced O Sensei that it was both necessary and important to do so. He successfully solicited support from many important people in the business and political communities in the difficult postwar years. He ran and maintained the organizational structure of Honbu Dojo and kept its operations smooth and efficient. He tirelessly taught at outlying dojo, at universities, and at businesses. He maintained harmony and cooperation among O Sensei's senior instructors and shihan, many of whom were people of strong temperament, opinions, and will, and he did so with great patience.

Most important, to him falls the added burden of passing on the teachings of O Sensei in the purest form possible. As Doshu once said to me, it is the right and the privilege of other shihan to embellish their understanding of Aikido with their own personal style and to bring their training and teaching knowledge acquired from their studies of other martial arts. Doshu, however, has the obligation, to

Doto: Successor

preserve the teachings of O Sensei lest their original meaning be lost. With unfailing humility and courtesy, Doshu has pursued this path. And yet in his iron will, his constant courage, and his strict discipline the inheritance of his father and of the Ueshiba family can be seen.

It would take a long time to name all of those whose hard work and dedication in both study and instruction have helped to further the growth of Aikido. Both in Japan and abroad, their efforts have been invaluable in the development and dissemination of the art of Aikido. But inherent in an art that demands such strong will and dedication are some serious problems, the effect of which can already be seen. Within the world community of Aikido, there has already been much competitiveness, much infighting for

ascendency; and many petty squabbles have occurred. It is time, I think, to look at the history of Aikido so far to remind ourselves of its purpose and to bring those who follow its path back into harmony. In the dedication and creativity of the founder, Morihei Ueshiba, for the cause of world peace and in the self-effacement and dedication of Doshu, his successor, we may see several lessons. Our goal is to pass on the spirit of Aikido, not to gratify our monetary greed or satisfy our egos. In order to create a new society, to educate its spirit to cope with its technology—which was O Sensei's wish—we must remember O Sensei's original prayers for peace. Without a center, Aikido will fall apart. We must return to the center, to O Sensei's teachings, to humility, cooperation, and harmony. If we do not, the spirit and the purpose of Aikido will be lost.

Glossary

Aiki   Universal life energy, the creative principle of life

Aikido   The art founded by Morihei Ueshiba O Sensei, the way of aiki

Aikidoka   One who practices Aikido

Aiki no kurai   The secret of aiki, the highest consciousness of aiki

Ai nuke   Mutual preservation

Ai uchi   Mutual destruction

Amaterasu (Omi Kami)   The goddess of the sun

Atemi   A strike to an opening

Atemiwaza   Atemi technique(s)

Bokken   Wooden practice sword

Bu   To stop weapons (literally, "to stop a spear"), war

Budo   The way of bu

Budoka   One who practices budo

Bujutsu   Fighting techniques

Bushi   Warrior

Bushido   The way of the warrior

Chi   Wisdom, intelligence

Chin kon ki shin   A practice intended to aid one in joining with the universal spirit and to help one understand the divine mission that it is one's life goal to fulfill

Chu   Loyalty

Chushin   One's center

Deshi   A follower, a student, a disciple

Do   The way

Do   A cut to the side

Dogi   Practice uniform

Dojo   Place where one studies a *do,* or way

Do-no-tanden   Middle-body training

Dori   Take, grab, grasp

Doshu   The person who shows the way, head of Aikido

Gi   Honor, justice

Giri   Cut

Hakama   Traditional pleated pants worn by the samurai and by kobudo students

Hanmi   The basic triangular stance of Aikido

Hara   One's center, the seat of one's life energy

Harigaya Usai Sekiun   A renowned seventeenth-century Japanese swordsman

Hijiri   Sage

Hoko   Spear, one of the component elements in the kanji *bu*

Honbu Dojo   The international headquarters of Aikido

Ichi   One, first

Ikkyo   The first movement, the first principle

Inazuma   Lightning

Irimi   The act of entering directly into the attack

Iriminage   A throw whose main element is irimi

Jin   Benevolence

Jiuwaza   Freestyle practice

Jo   The five-foot wooden staff

Kaeshiwaza   Reversal technique(s)

Kagura mai   Dance of the gods

Kaitenage   Spinning throw

Kami   God(s)

Kanji   Chinese characters, ideographs

Kannagara no michi   Way of the Japanese emperor and of the gods

Kata   Set form(s)

Katadori   Shoulder grab(s)

Katatedori   Wrist grab(s)

Katsu jin ken   The saving of your enemy's life

Kazumi Ise no Kami Nobutsena   Founder of the Shin Kage sword school

Keiko   Practice

Ken   Sword

Kendo   The modern art of Japanese fencing

Kenjutsu   Sword techniques

Kesa giri   Diagonal cut across the body

Ki   Life energy

Kobudo   Classical Japanese martial arts

Koh   Piety

Kohai   Junior student

Kojiki   Japanese myths of origin

Kokyu   Breath or breathing as cyclic energy

Kokyu tanden ho   An exercise in musubi, in blending the rhythm of your vital energies with those of your partner

Kosadori   Cross-hand grab

Koshinage   Hip throw

Kotegaeshi   Wrist twist

Kote giri   Wrist cut

Kotodama   Spiritual sounds

Kumiiai   Paired sword practice in which both partners begin with their swords still sheathed, in part practice in the art of drawing swords

Kumi tachi   Paired sword practice in which both partners begin with their swords already drawn

Ku no ji giri   Cut in the shape of the character *ku*

Kurai   Secret, consciousness, inner being

Kurai dori   To control another's consciousness

Kyu   Grades preceding yudansha rank

Meiji Restoration   The period following the advent of Admiral Perry, in which Japan began the process of modernization

Michi   Way

Misogi   Cleansing, spiritual cleansing

Misogi harai   Actions that realize misogi

Miyamoto Musashi   One of Japan's greatest and most renowned swordsmen, author of *The Book of Five Rings*

Mu   Void

Munetsuki   Strike or thrust to the middle body

Musubi   Harmonious connection, unity, ultimately our unity with all life and with the universe

Nage   A throw, one who throws

Nikyo   Second technique, a technique that uses wrist torque to control the opponent's center

Omote   To the front

O Sensei   Great Teacher

Randori   Multiple attack practice

Rei   Etiquette, courtesy

Reigi   Etiquette, courtesy

Ryotemochi   Two-hand grab (either two hands grabbing one hand or two hands grabbing two hands)

Ryu   Style or school of practice, as in "Daito ryu jujutsu"

Samurai   One who serves

Sankyo   Third technique, control of the opponent's center through the wrist and elbow

Satori   Enlightenment, epiphany

Satsu jin ken   The destruction or killing of one's enemy

Seiza   Traditional Japanese manner of sitting with one's knees folded under one

Sempai   Senior student

Sensei   Teacher, one who gives guidance along the way, one who goes before

Shihan   Master teacher

Shihan-dai   Designated representative(s) of a shihan

Shihonage   Four-corner throw

Shikko   Traditional manner of walking on one's knees

Shin   Sincerity

Shinto   Way of the Gods, traditional religion of Japan

Shomen   The head, a cut or strike to the front of the head

Shomenuchi   Specifically, an empty hand strike to the front of the head with the blade of the hand

Shuto   A sharp strike with the blade of the hand

Suburi   Repetitions of a motion done in order to perfect performance

Suki   Openings, weak points

Suwariwaza   Technique(s) performed in seiza and shikko

Tachi   Sword

Tachidori   Sword taking

Tatami   Traditional Japanese straw mats

Teji Kara no Mikoto   The god of incomparable strength

Tenkan   Turning movement used to dissipate force

Todomeru   To stop, one of the component elements in the kanji *bu*

Tsuki   A thrust or punch

Uchi deshi   Personal student or disciple

Ude osai   Control of the center through the arm

Ueshiba Morihei   The founder of Aikido

Ueshiba Kisshomaru   The current doshu, O Sensei's son

Uke   The one who receives the force, the person who is thrown

Ukemi   The art of being an uke

Ura   To the rear

Ushirowaza   Technique(s) in which one is attacked from behind

Waza   Techniques

Yokomen   Strike or cut to the side of the head or neck

Yokomenuchi   Specifically, an empty hand strike to the side of the head or neck with the blade of the hand

Yonkyo   Fourth technique, control of the opponent's center through his wrist, elbow, and shoulder

Yudansha   Those who have achieved dan, or black belt, ranking in an art

Yukoku no shi   Noble guardians of a nation, another term for samurai

Zanshin   The complete and continuous awareness of one's surroundings

About the Author

Mitsugi Saotome was a personal disciple of Morihei Ueshiba for fifteen years until the Founder's death in 1969. In 1975 Saotome Sensei left a highly respected position as a senior instructor at the World Aikido Headquarters in Tokyo to come to the United States. When asked why he made this decision, he replied, "I meditated on O Sensei's spirit for three days and three nights, and I felt it was his wish that I should go. O Sensei spoke to me of this before his death. The eyes of the world are on the United States. This country is a great experiment, a melting pot of people from different cultural backgrounds living together, the world condensed into one nation. The goal of Aikido and O Sensei's dream is that all the people of the world live together as one family, in harmony with each other and with their environment. The United States has the opportunity to set a great example."

Saotome Sensei spends most of his time at his headquarters dojo in Washington, D.C. He also travels to associated dojos of the Aikido Schools of Ueshiba, which he and his students have opened throughout the country, as well as to Europe, to lead seminars and training camps. He has given many demonstrations of his art both in the United States and abroad, including demonstrations for the International Peace Academy and Diplomatic Community at Japan House in New York City.

The address of the Washington, D.C., dojo is as follows:

The Washington D.C. Aikikai
421 Butternut Street, N.W.
Washington, DC 20012

Tel.: (202) 829-4202